ESSENTIAL

SURFING

*To Scott.
Good Luck &
Good Waves.
George Orbelian
10·88*

GEORGE
ORBELIAN

SURFBOARD DESIGN EDITOR **SURFER** MAGAZINE

Published by:

Orbelian Arts
417 Dewey Boulevard
San Francisco, CA 94116   ISBN 0-9610548-2-4

Cover Design & Illustration: George Orbelian. **Illustrations:** George Bredehoft.
Typesetting: Graphico, San Francisco

This book is dedicated to my wife, Marcia
and my sons, Craig and Wade

For many surfers there comes a time when riding the ocean's waves becomes more important than just having great fun...when our beaches, points and reefs become what wetlands are to wildlife— essential habitat.

The Surfrider Foundation is a California based, non-profit organization of men and women who are dedicated to the protection and enjoyment of our ocean waves and beaches worldwide. Preserving our natural beaches, working to enhance ocean wave recreation; defending public access, water quality and marine ecology are what The Surfrider Foundation is about.

"Every citizen has the responsibility to contribute to the preservation and enhancement of the environment."
—California Environmental Quality Act, 1970

If those who love the sea don't protect her—who will?

The Surfrider Foundation, a non-profit organization
P.O. Box 2704 #86
Huntington Beach, California 82647
(714) 846-3462

Special Thanks to George Bredehoft, the Burns family, Duncan & Malcom Campbell, Gordon Clark (Clark Foam), Mike Eaton, Laura Kruszynski, Dick Morales, Harry & Vera Orbelian, Brigid Oversmith, Rym Partridge, Marcia Paulsen, Sarah Pearce, Bob Pettijohn (Gerisch Products, Inc.), Robin Prodanovich, Greg Raymond, Craig & Brenda Rogers, Doctor Scott, Steve Seebold, SURFER Magazine staff, Fred Van Dyke, and Bob Wise.

Table of Contents

List of Illustrations

Preface

I have been surfing for many years, and spent seven years working for Wise Surfboards in San Francisco. During that time I answered the same questions over and over again. The beginners needed basic information about learning how to surf, the ways of the ocean, and the type of board easiest to learn on. More advanced surfers were concerned with surfboard design, so they could choose the board that would best suit their styles. I found it wasn't always possible to spend as much time as I would have liked with each customer. Some questions led to hours of involved discussion with surfboards all over the floor. Often though, due to the needs of other customers, there wasn't time to adequately explain. The rise in petro-chemical prices and inflation have increased the prices of surfing equipment, making it even more important to make the right choice.

I decided to write this book so that people interested in surfing and surfing equipment could have a reference of basic information essential to safe and intelligent involvement in the sport. I have done my best to provide the most accurate and up to date information available. All the information presented here is backed by experience. I'm in the water as often as possible, pushing my abilities and equipment. Constantly trying new designs gives me insight into the surfboard design/surfer performance relationship. I have personally built several of the ninety surfboards I have owned through the years and spent many hours discussing surfboard design with professional shapers and experienced surfers.

After reviewing of a review copy of ESSENTIAL SURFING, SURFER Magazine asked me to join their staff as Surfboard Design Editor. Working with the magazine has exposed me to many different shapers as well as to the latest breakthroughs in surfboard design. In addition I answer questions from readers which keeps me in touch with the type of information surfers are interested in. I'm stoked that surfers are becoming increasingly aware of the influence that equipment has on their surfing performance and ultimately their enjoyment of the sport.

I owe a great deal of thanks to friends who have taken time discussing ideas, reading through manuscripts and offering information and inspiration. As designs evolve and new materials are developed, I plan to update this book so it will remain an accurate source of information about available equipment. If you have any questions or comments about ideas that were or weren't covered feel free to write.

Types of Surfing

Bodysurfing – Just a body and a wave. Usually bodysurfing is done with the aid of swim fins to help the bodysurfer generate the necessary speed to catch the wave. Once the wave has been caught the body actually becomes the planing surface. Skillful bodysurfers are capable of extraordinary rides and maneuvers. Some masters can actually ride the *"energy"* just beneath the face of the wave, without ever actually protruding out of the wave. You may come across seals or dolphins enjoying waves by bodysurfing with their uncanny skill.

Belly / Bodyboarding – Bodysurfing with the aid of a planing device. The planing device may be small and hand held, planing out once the bodysurfer catches a wave. The larger, soft, flexible bodyboards have inspired a new sport. The bodyboard is small and easy to manage while affording substantial floatation and planing ability. These qualities assist the prone, swim fin assisted rider in catching and riding waves. Bodyboards come in a wide variety of shapes, with varying degrees of flex / stiffness and many different fin / rail configurations. expert bodyboarders are capable of amazing rides. Their prone position lends them stability as well as allowing them to fit in the tight confines of a deep tube. Occasionally they kneel or stand on their bodyboards while performing a particular maneuver. The best riders go out and rip at Pipeline – their potential should not be underestimated.

Note: Both bodysurfing and bellyboarding are excellent presurfing interests. They familiarize one with the ocean and waves. Wave judgement is the most difficult aspect of surfing to master. The actual balance of riding a board isn't that difficult for people to learn, but before you can ride waves you have to catch waves. Every surf spot will have its own characteristic wave which will change according to tide, swell, and wind. It takes years to accumulate the experience needed to deal with the multitude of situations the sea is capable of. You may find that bodysurfing and bellyboarding provide you with the thrill you were searching for. If you decide to kneeboard or surf, the wave judgement learned while bodysurfing or bellyboarding will be an invaluable asset to your progress.

Kneeboarding – A type of surfing where the surfer rides a specialized board on his knees. Most kneeboards are tri or quad fin designs between five and six feet in length. Padded chest or double knee wells are utilized on some kneeboards to improve control and surfing performance. Swim fins are worn to help propel the small boards into waves. Kneeboarding allows the rider to get into a very compact and stable position. The small board and stance of the kneeboarder make this type of surfing very suitable for steep drops, quick radical maneuvers and tube riding.

Surfing – Surfing is the sport of riding across the face of a wave while standing on a specialized board. Surfing takes place on waves from one foot to over thirty feet in height. Surfing originated in Hawaii and was introduced to the world by the legendary Hawaiian waterman, Duke Kahanamoku.

Early surfboards were made of solid wood, up to sixteen feet in length, and weighed up to one hundred and thirty pounds. They had no fin on the bottom and were turned by dragging a foot in the face of the wave.

Boards and surfing performance evolved simultaneously. As fins and lighter materials such as balsa wood, foam and fiberglass were used in construction, the potential for maneuverability increased. Current boards range from five and one-half feet to twelve feet long. Short foam boards with ultra-light fiberglass shells weigh as little as six pounds. Longboards recreated by master shapers and stylists that made them in the sixties utilize traditional or contemporary design specifications. Single and multi-fin configurations are utilized to achieve desired performance characteristics.

Surfing styles and equipment have evolved to very specialized extremes. Surfers have available to them a wider variety of refined equipment than ever before. Many enjoy developing the ability to surf well on diverse designs. Personal preference, wave conditions, and the objectives of one's surfing dictate the type of approach and equipment most suitable.

Tandem Surfing – Surfing with a partner on the same board. An extra-wide surfboard which is nine feet or longer is used for increased stability and to compensate for the added weight of two riders. Usually a surfer carries a woman or lofts her on his shoulders where she performs a series of graceful poses.

Windsurfing – Windsurfing was developed in the late sixties by Hoyle

Schweitzer. The sport utilizes a board that is rigged with a mast, boom, sail and footstraps. Boards vary in length from eight to twelve feet depending on design objectives, the sailors size, experience, and the wind conditions the board will be used in. Many surfboard designers/shapers and craftsmen got into building high performance sailboards. Since design ideas and construction techniques were so well refined, sailboards enjoyed a very rapid design evolution. Small boards are favored for sailing and jumping amongst waves. They require a "water start" (using the sail to support your weight to facilitate acceleration to planing speed) and are fast and maneuverable. Expert sailors can outrun incredible sections and using waves for ramps, launch themselves high into the air, whip a loop and use their sail as a wing to ease their descent. As of this writing a sailboard holds the world speed record (at over 40 m.p.h) making it the fastest sailing craft on the water.

Skimboarding – Skimboarding is a sport that combines the art of surfing, the agility and maneuvering of skateboarding and the graceful flair of diving. Skimboards resemble small surfboards and range in size from 18" x 35" to 24" x 48". They are available in various shapes, and are built from laminated marine plywood, fiberglass and foam depending on the preference of the rider. Skimboarders run along the shoreline, pass their boards onto the thin layer of water expended by the shorebreak onto the beach, and jump on, their boards skimming (planing) upon this thin layer of water. As skills develop they are able to maintain speed and continue into cresting shorebreak waves, catapulting onto the air, spinning around and landing back on the board.

Introduction to Surfboard Design Terminology

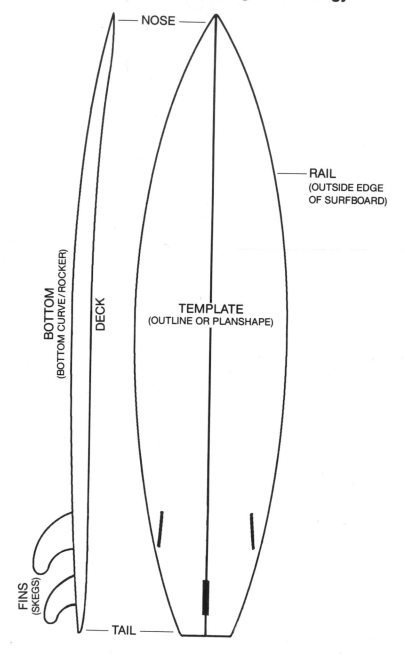

NOSE

RAIL
(OUTSIDE EDGE
OF SURFBOARD)

BOTTOM
(BOTTOM CURVE / ROCKER)

DECK

TEMPLATE
(OUTLINE OR PLANSHAPE)

FINS
(SKEGS)

TAIL

Introduction to Surfboard Design

Good equipment is essential to a surfer. A surfboard that works well for you will make a tremendous difference in how much you enjoy the sport, how quickly you progress, and the level of ability you can attain. Every handbuilt surfboard is unique. There are many design elements a shaper incorporates into every board, and fractions of an inch can make a noticeable difference in their effect on performance. Surfers are lucky in that they have a chance to influence the design of their equipment and develop boards that will compliment their styles and the waves they normally encounter. The information in this book will give any surfer an improved understanding of design and it's effect on performance characteristics, enabling him to take full advantage of a shaper. Understanding design enhances your ability to communicate with a shaper and improve your equipment.

The top professional shapers have shaped thousands of boards. They spend a great deal of time refining designs and accumulating feedback about boards they've made. Surfboard design is a complex association of many variables. The shaper is engineer, craftsman and artist. Templates and measurements are used to benefit accuracy, with the eyes and hands insuring consistency. The shaper is free to blend particular design elements to create specific performance characteristics. Customized equipment and the rapid assimilation and refinement of new designs are the benefits of individually hand-crafted construction.

A great deal of the appeal of a surfboard is aesthetic. If it appeals to you and your friends you'll be stoked. If you're stoked, you're going to surf better. Try not to confuse aesthetic features with functional ones. Rather, appreciate features in a shape that correspond to the type of performance you want from the board.

The best surfboard does not exist. One look at the pros will illustrate that surfers of the same ability use a wide variety of equipment while competing in similar conditions, in an effort to impress the same judging system. As long as you're stoked and having fun, you're on the right equipment.

A good surfer isn't going to go against the grain of his experience and keep a board that doesn't feel right. That's why you'll sometimes find virtually brand new boards in the used board rack.

Shapers generally agree on the effects particular design features have on performance; however there are an infinite number of ways to combine design features to satisfy the requirements of a particular surfer, wave or design objective. Shaper Mike Eaton shared the following insight with me; when thinking of template and rocker curves, straighter longer lines on a board result in longer more drawn out turns and shorter rounder curves result in a sharper, rounder turning characteristic. Most design elements built into surfboards are a delicate balance between speed and control. Design elements that make a surfboard faster, make it more difficult to control and the features that make a surfboard turn easier, slow it down. The quest of the shaper is to combine design elements so a board utilizes wave energy efficiently, converting it to speed, yet maintains a responsive and positive turning characteristic. Eaton game me some other good advice - never sell a board that you really like. I'll add to that - until you find one that you like better; I've put this information together to make the search easier for you - good luck.

Longboards

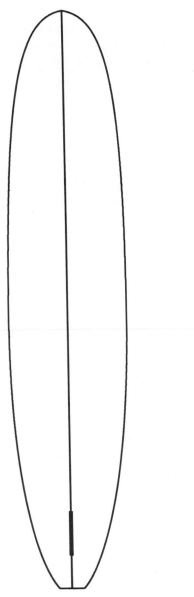

Lance Carson
Traditional Longboard
9'6"x22" 16 1/2"N 15"T

Stewart
Competition Longboard
9'0"x22 1/2" 18 1/4"N 13 1/4"T
shading indicates concaves

7

Types of Surfboards

Longboards – Boards of classic design that are typically 8′6″ to 9′6″ in length, with some boards even longer. Competition rules typically specify that a longboard must be at least three feet longer than the height of the surfer competing on it. Longboards are available in a wide variety of styles utilizing everything from traditional designs with single fin configurations and heavier weight glass jobs to progressive competition models that utilize the latest design innovations, multi-fin configurations and ultra light glass jobs. Shorter hybrid "fun boards," "egg" designs, and "mini" longboards in the 7′0″ to 8′6″ length combine design features of both long and short boards.

Purpose: The increased length of a longboard allows it to glide. When paddling, you glide between strokes which helps you paddle faster with less effort so it's easier to catch waves. The ability of the longboard to maintain momentum is one of the main reasons the design is so well suited to small or marginal surf that is riddled with flat spots. Superior flotation and increased width improve low speed planing efficiency and stability. The shorter hybrids offer these attributes in a shorter, more maneuverable design.

Single Fin – The single fin is the basic surfboard and has been built in a full range of lengths, utilizing a wide variety of template designs. Single fins have been experimented with and refined throughout the evolution of surfboard design. They have been adapted to ride all sizes of surf. The tri fin has been the first concept in the history of surfboard design to successfully challenge the versatility of the single fin.

Purpose: The single fin utilizes one fin that is located directly over the midline of the tail. This gives it a very neutral turning characteristic.

Gun – A big wave board made for waves eight feet and larger in single or tri fin configurations. A common misconception is that the gun board is the fastest design of all. Actually, gun boards are built for control utilizing design features that are inherently slow. In addition to longer overall lengths, guns utilize proportionally narrower templates, increased rocker, softer rails and substantial amounts of "V" and belly to maintain control in the higher speeds common to larger surf.

Purpose: The gun board is made to deal with the higher speeds, chop, bump and currents common to larger surf. The longer length makes paddling easier and allows you to get into waves earlier. It also increases the length of the rail line (edge of the surfboard) so there is more edge in the face of the wave. The narrower template dimensions reduce planing area, improving stability at higher speeds and enhancing control on steep drops. Increased rocker, softer rails, "V" (in the tail) and belly (in the nose) make the gun easier to lean on edge and turn at higher speeds.

Twin Fin - A short board (usually 5'8"-6'8") with a wide tail for maneuverability and a fin near each rail for stability in radical turns. This design is especially well suited to smaller surf (under 6 feet), but has been pushed into mid-sized Hawaiian surf by shaper/four time world champion surfer Mark Richards (Australia).

Purpose: A wider tail area provides more planing area and lift which creates more speed by efficiently utilizing wave energy. *Milking* speed and energy from small surf with extremely sensitive and responsive turning ability are this design's strong points.

Bonzer - Originally designed by the Campbell brothers and refined for many years by Mike Eaton, the bonzer is one of the most complex surfboard designs ever offered on a production level. The double concaves shaped into the tail area can be used in conjunction with a multitude of templates and bottom contours. The bonzer concaves work in conjunction with short, angled ventral fins placed at the outside edge of the concave. A short raked center fin is also used.

Purpose: The Venturi principle is applied to achieve greater speed and acceleration. The ventral fins are essential to control water flow and enhance maneuverability.

Tri Fin/Thruster - A three fin design utilizing a specialized template. The template usually incorporates increased tail width. The wide point is located at or within a few inches of center. The nose is on the narrow side. The two side fins are toed in, canted out and placed near the rail like the fins on a twin fin. The third fin is set two to four inches from the tip of the tail. The performance characteristics of the thruster are closely associated with its specialized template. The three fin system is being used on longer boards with narrower templates for adaptation to larger, faster, and more powerful surf.

Purpose: The thruster design evolved from the dissatisfaction Simon Anderson (Australia) had with the twin fin. When radically

Types of Surfboards

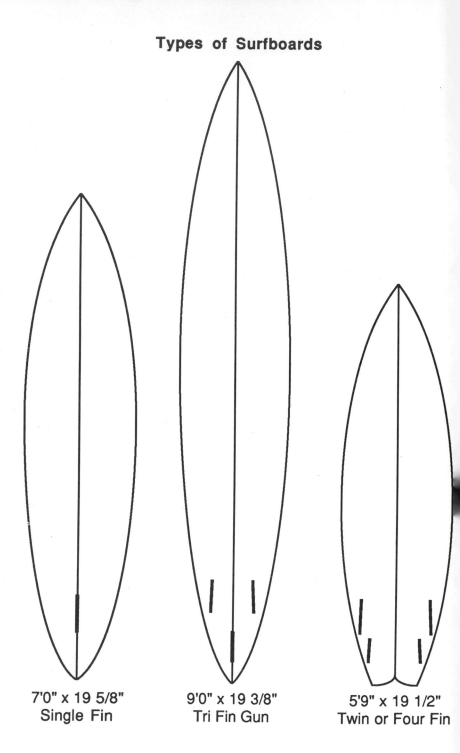

7'0" x 19 5/8"
Single Fin

9'0" x 19 3/8"
Tri Fin Gun

5'9" x 19 1/2"
Twin or Four Fin

carving on a twin fin, because the tail is so wide, one fin gets out of the water. This leaves a wide tail with a relatively small fin area straining to control the turning force. Some feel this is the reason the twins drift sideways, losing forward projection on radical turns. The thruster adds a small fin back on the tail to deal with forceful turns and improve tracking and projection. With the wide point at or very close to center, the wide tail and extremely narrow nose; the majority of this surfboard's area is directly beneath the surfer. The wide tail is very loose and fast; holding in well because of the three fins. The minimal area of the narrow nose offers very little resistance to the maneuvering surfer because there is very little weight to swing around and there are no edges to hang up. Fin location, templates, length, and rocker curves are constantly refined for various conditions. The tri-fin design has been very successful in large, powerful waves, and is the design of choice for Oahu's North Shore.

Four Fin – A short board (usually 5'8" to 6'8") the four fin adds fin area to eliminate the drift and slide characteristic to twin fins. The four fin utilizes a wide tail for efficient planing (and enhanced maneuverability) at low speeds. Two fins near each rail provide control during radical turns. The four fin provides more drive and projection than a twin fin and is looser rail to rail than a tri fin.

Purpose: The four fin design places fins near the rails where they can do the most good when the board is leaned on edge. The forward set of fins are further up than they would be on a twin fin and smaller. The rear set of fins are inboard and behind the front set. The rear set is shorter, so that even tough they are closer together than the forward set, they still leave the water when the board is leaned on edge. The four fin is more positive and has more drive and projection out of turns than a twin because it has more fin area in the water. The four fin is looser and goes edge to edge quicker than the tri fin because the center fin on the tri fin always remains in the water.

Hydro Hull – The hydro hull was inspired by the hull designs utilized on hydro plane racing boats. Bill Stewart transfered the design concepts to a surfboard. The hydro hull is a combination of increased "V", subtle double concaves and double edged chine rails, compatable with a wide variety of lengths and template designs.

Types of Surfboards

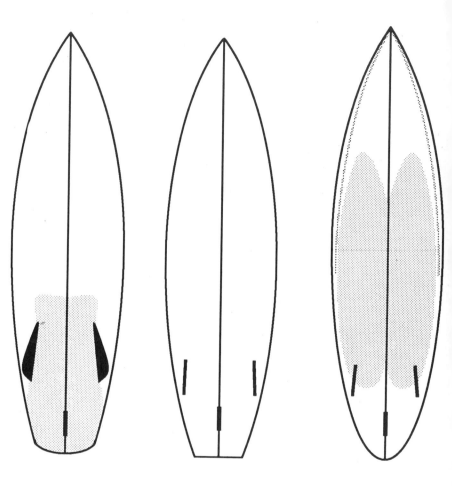

6'2" x 19"
Bonzer
shading indicates concaves

6'0" x 19 1/2"
Tri Fin

6'3" x 19 1/2"
Hydro-Hull
shading indicates concave

Purpose: The hydro hull bottom incorporates increased "V" for quick rail to rail transitions. A double edged rail facilitates release while maintaining a nose to tail edge for bite and projection. A subtle double concave is added which creates a straighter, faster rocker as well as providing increased lift which dramatically improves planing efficiency. With this design your front foot drives off of the concaves while your rear foot utilizes flat "V" panels in the tail area for a loose turning characteristic. Stewart recommends going longer and narrower when switching to his hydro hulls because of the dramatic improvement in planing efficiency.

Template Dimensions

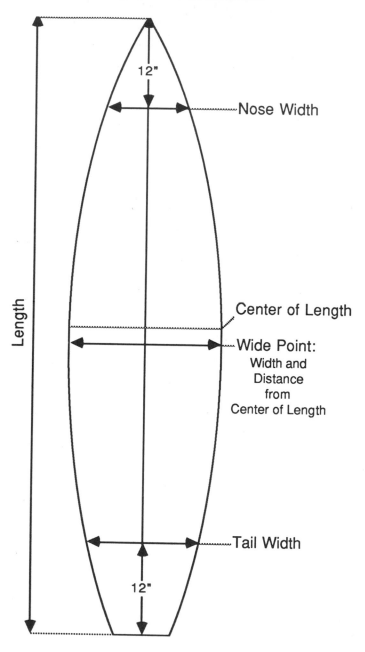

12"

Nose Width

Center of Length

Wide Point:
Width and
Distance
from
Center of Length

Length

Tail Width

12"

Surfboard Design Terminology and Function

Note: Whenever possible, measure all dimensions on the bottom. Shapers plot measurements and template curves on the bottom when designing a board. Since the bottom is flatter than the deck, one can sight the outside edge of the rail with greater accuracy.

It is difficult to isolate and compare various design features of a surfboard. As length or width change, knowledgable shapers compensate by adjusting rocker, bottom contours, the placement of the wide point, the types of rails, and the number of fins, etc. By the use of specialized design features shapers can "*set up*" boards, short or long, for various conditions. A short board for large fast surf, a long board for small slow surf or visa versa. In the following examples, I'll be comparing hypothetical boards that are set up for and ridden in the same type of surf, the only difference being the design feature in question. Everything else about the boards is as similar as possible, so that you can get an idea how the particular design feature influences performance.

As you pay closer attention to the designs of the boards you ride, you will gain practical experience as to the way in which various design features influence your surfing. The ability to identify various design features and understand how they influence performance, will help you evaluate surfboards and communicate with shapers more effectively. If you are considering a new board, knowledge of design will help you pick the board that suits you best.

Template/Planshape–The outline curve or silhouette of the surfboard. The template should be the smoothest most flowing line that will accommodate dimensions for a specific design and length. Longer, straighter template curves which result in a template that has a more parallel nature usually result in boards that perform longer, straighter, more drawn out turns. Rounder, curvy templates are usually more suited to rounder, sharper turns.

Length–The total length of the board from the tip of the nose to the tip(s) of the tail.
Function: The longer board will provide more flotation than a shorter board because it contains more foam. A longer board will paddle easier and catch waves earlier than a shorter board. Longer boards glide, carry speed, and keep momentum up through slow or

mushy sections of a wave better than shorter boards. As the length of the rail line is increased, control is improved. For this reason, longer boards are more stable than shorter boards in big, bumpy and fast surf. Shorter boards turn easier, quicker, and are more maneuverable than longer boards. Shorter boards fit into the tight confines of smaller waves more readily and are more sensitive to front/rear weight transfer than longer boards. One asset of this sensitivity, is that it makes it easier to negotiate steep drops in small surf without pearling. The characteristics of shorter boards enable the surfer to generate speed by quickly weighting and unweighting to maneuver through critical sections of a wave.

Width – The widest point of the template. Most boards are between 18½″ and 22″ in width. Depending on the design of the surfboard, the wide point may be located anywhere from five inches behind center, to eight inches ahead of center.

Function: The wider board contains more foam, which enhances floatation. Wider boards paddle easier and catch waves earlier. The increased planing area efficiently utilizes energy from small and slow waves providing more speed than available with a narrow board. The added speed improves maneuverability because the board is planing freely rather than dragging through the water.

Narrow boards have less planing area than wide boards which suits them to big and fast waves, where there is an overabundance of energy and control is the primary design objective.

At higher speeds, excessive width makes a board difficult to control. The board will skitter, drift, slide and resist being leaned on edge. As speeds increase, planing area can be reduced – as illustrated by a barefoot water skier. Boards built for faster waves (like Oahu's North Shore) are narrower so they'll stay down in the water and carve; improving control at higher speeds. Narrower boards are favored by competition surfers because they go rail to rail quicker.

The location of the wide point influences a board's turning characteristic. The further ahead of center the wide point is placed, the longer and more drawn out the board's turns will become. Moving the wide point back, near or behind the center of the board, makes the board turn quicker and sharper.

Nose Width–Measure 12″ from the tip of the nose.

Function: The proportionally wider nose contains more foam which provides better flotation. The board with the wider nose is going to paddle easier which will make it easier to catch waves. The additional planing area is an advantage in small or slow surf. The wider nose will resist sinking and slowing down when the surfer moves forward on the board. Extremely wide noses set up with very little nose kick and/or concaves are used for nose riding.

Narrow noses are used on big wave boards (guns) so that offshore winds won't hang the surfer up at the crest of the wave as he attempts to catch it. Some surfers feel that the minimal mass and area of the narrow nose enhances maneuverability.

Tail Width–Measure 12″ from the tip(s) of the tail.

Function: The wider tail contains more foam than the narrow tail, which aids flotation, paddling, and wave catching ability. The additional planing area of a wide tail enhances low speed response, maneuverability, and stability. Increased planing area utilizes as much speed as possible from slow, mushy and small surf. The wider tail will feel freer, looser, and more maneuverable at low speeds than the narrow tail. As tail width (and area) is increased, additional fin area is required to maintain control. Fin area is increased by the use of a larger fin or by utilizing a multi-fin design.

The narrow tail is used on boards made for big, fast, and hollow surf where there is an overabundance of energy and control is the primary design objective. The minimal planing area of the narrow tail makes it easier to turn and more stable at high speeds.

Full Template–A template that is dimensionally wider than normal.

Function: Superior for beginners, very stable, suited to slow or small surf.

Pulled Template–A template that is dimensionally narrower than normal. Also referred to as a "gunny" (like a gun) template.

Function: Superior for large or fast, steep surf where there is an overabundance of energy and control is of primary importance. Like a waterski, these boards don't really feel loose (maneuverable) until they reach a certain speed. Once that energy is available, they become a necessity.

Templates

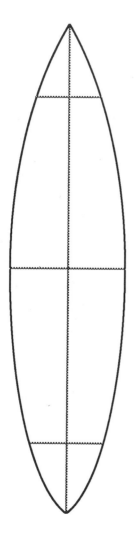

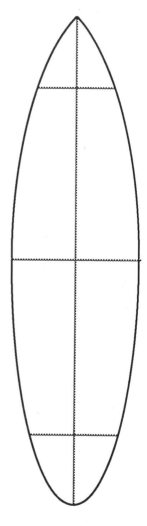

Pulled Template
7'0" x 18 3/4"

Full Template
7'0" x 20 3/4"

Rails

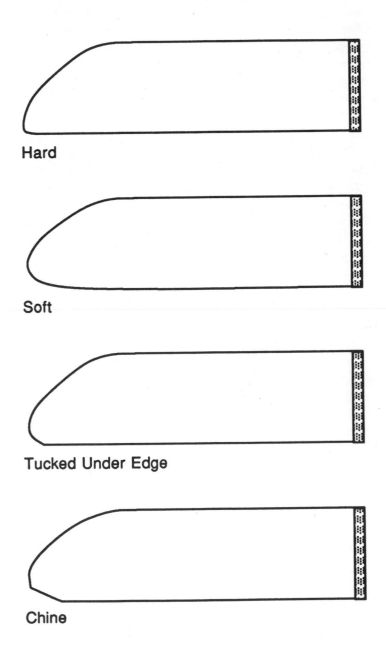

Hard

Soft

Tucked Under Edge

Chine

Rail - The outside edge of the surfboard.
Function: Fuller rails carry more foam. This aids response because of resistance to sinking and stalling when leaned on edge. Thinner, tapered rails carry less foam, making them easier to sink and lean on edge. The harder the edge, the cleaner the water breaks away and releases from the board, which contributes to speed and looseness. Hard rails penetrate the water poorly at high speeds and resist being leaned on edge. Softer rails provide a smoother, more forgiving response than hard rails. The water tends to bend around their subtle curve rather than breaking away. The bigger the waves you want the board to work in, the softer the rails should be. A very popular design feature is the tucked under edge. This design gives you the clean water release of a hard rail with the penetration and holding power of a softer rail. Hard rail edges are utilized in the tail area for improved release with control maintained by the fins. Chine rails utilize an additional ridge or edge that improves the shapers ability to control the bite and release points of a rail. Most boards use a combination of rail configurations.

Rocker - The bottom curve of the surfboard This curve is most apparent when the board is laid upon a flat surface.
Function: Rocker is probably the single most important factor which determines how a surfboard works. The curve of the rocker will carve a particular arc when the board is leaned over in a turn. If the rocker is very full or round, the board will turn a tight, sharp arc. If the rocker is straighter or flatter, the board will carve a larger radius or more drawn out turn. Some shapers design the rocker to be a very smooth continuous curve, whereas other shapers fit the rocker that will perform best when the surfer is standing over a particular portion of it. Where one stands on the surfboard determines what part of the rocker is engaged with the wave. This is why boards have a sweet spot - a place which, when stood over, feels comfortable and allows for ultimate maneuvering.

Flatter rocker is faster, paddles easier, and catches waves earlier. Flatter rocker creates a longer, more drawn out turning characteristic with down the line drive. Flatter rocker makes a board more difficult to turn and easier to pearl.

Fuller rocker is slower, paddles worse, and catches waves later. The more pronounced curve pushes the water ahead of it like a plow rather than skimming up on top of it. Fuller, rounder rocker creates a shorter, tighter and rounder turning characteristic. Fuller rocker creates a looser turning characteristic and is more resistant to pearling.

Usually as the length of the board increases the rocker increases, and as the length decreases the rocker decreases. Shorter boards can get by with less rocker for several reasons; their shorter length allows them to turn easily; they fit into a tigher curve in the face of the wave without pearling; and they are more responsive to front/rear weight transfer.

A board with too much rocker will be inherently slow, with a very loose turning characteristic. Boards with increased rocker work best in steep, fast, powerful waves. A board that doesn't have enough rocker will be inherently fast, with a very stiff turning characteristic. Boards with decreased rocker work best in slow, mushy waves.

Thin boards can get by with less rocker for they will actually flex (increasing their rocker) when they are pushed through turns yet maintain the benefits of flatter, faster rocker when unweighted.

Bill Barnfield utilizes a technique for measuring rocker that is used throughout the industry:
1. Turn the board bottom side up, measure it's total length and divide this measurement in half. Mark the exact center point of the board.
2. Balance a straight edge that's longer than the board and extends beyond both nose and tail directly upon your center mark. Set the straight edge directly over the stringer. To accommodate a glassed on rear fin, shift the straight edge to one side for clearance, keeping it parallel to the stringer.
3. Measure from the tip of the nose to the bottom edge of the straight edge (the edge resting on the board) to record the nose rocker.
4. Measure from the tip(s) of the tail to the bottom edge of the straight edge to record the tail rocker.

It is important that the straight edge is true and straight, for any sag will throw off your measurement. If you have trouble getting the straight edge to balance directly over the center mark, gently wedge a pencil under the straight edge to adjust the point where it touches the board. For a more detailed record of the rocker take a measurement every six inches.

Rocker Measurement Points

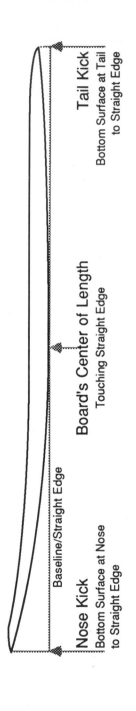

Baseline/Straight Edge

Board's Center of Length
Touching Straight Edge

Tail Kick
Bottom Surface at Tail
to Straight Edge

Nose Kick
Bottom Surface at Nose
to Straight Edge

Nose Kick – Nose kick refers to the upward curve or rocker in the front third of the board. Nose kick helps keep the board from pearling, and is the transition point that introduces water to the remainder of the bottom curve. Insufficient kick will cause the board to pearl while excessive kick will push water and slow the board down.

Tail Kick – Tail kick refers to the upward curve or rocker in the rear third of the board. The amount of rocker curve in the tail often increases noticeably immediately beyond the fins. This feature allows the surfer to bring the board around in a tight radius if necessary because the accentuated curve will carve a tighter arc with less resistance. If a shaper uses a straighter faster rocker in the middle of the board for speed, he can still give the surfer an option of turning very sharply by shaping accentuated kick into the tail. Interestingly, tail kick has more influence on pearling than nose kick does. By shifting the weight to the rear, a surfer can keep the nose of the board extremely light to prevent pearling. Tail kick facilitates rearward weight transfer.

Thickness Flow/Foil

Nose

Middle

Tail

Thickness Flow/Foil

The thickness flow, or foil, refers to the distribution of foam from the nose to the tail while looking at the side of the board.

Consider the board as being divided into three parts: the front third or nose; the middle third, which supports your torso when paddling; and, the rear third or tail area. The transition between these areas should be very smooth and flowing. Varying the amount of foam in a particular area will alter the way the board reacts and performs. The thickness of the rails should be even and consistent from side to side. Experienced shapers can feel and sight blanks with amazing accuracy. Any asymmetrical or unfunctional dips or bumps apparent to an uneducated eye would be an indication of an unprofessional shape job.

Boards should be matched to your body weight. Take into account that a wet full wetsuit weighs about nine pounds. The thickness of a board is essential for support while paddling, catching waves, and riding through slow or flat spots. The faster the wave moves you, the less thickness you can get by with.

Nose thickness – Some surfers feel that thinner noses react faster to turning input. With a thinner nose there is less weight at the nose that the surfer has to swing when turning.

If the rails just ahead of the wide point are too thin, they sink into the face of the wave when the surfer moves forward in trim. This causes the board to pivot around the wide point. When this occurs it causes the tail area to release from the face of the wave which results in slide or drift and disrupts control.

Middle thickness – The thickness of the middle part of the board should be set according to weight or preference.

Most boards are between 2¼" – 3¼" thick. If your weight or preference demands more floatation, width is added to the template dimensions.

A board that is too thin will paddle and catch waves poorly. When paddled, or ridden at low speeds, excessively thin boards feel sluggish as though they are dragging through the water.

A thick board will paddle and catch waves easily. When ridden, excessively thick boards may feel excessively buoyant, making them resistant to being leaned on edge and difficult to control. Thicker boards are stiffer and less likely to break in half than thinner boards.

Tail thickness – Thicker tails make the board paddle and catch waves easier. Thicker tails turn more easily and carry speed in slow, small surf better because they don't sink and drag.

Thinner tails provide more positive control. They hold in better in fast and hollow surf.

With single fins one limitation a shaper has when shaping tail thickness involves the fin box. The box is about one inch thick and its rear edge should be no further than six inches from the tip of the tail. If your weight or preference demand a really thin tail, get a glassed on fin.

Deck Contour – The deck contour refers to the shape of the deck 90° to the stringer. Some shapers utilize flat decks while others use a domed (also referred to as crowned or rounded) deck contour. Most contemporary boards have fairly flat decks because of thin overall thicknesses utilized in conjunction with full, boxy rails. This keeps the thickness quite uniform from rail to rail, resulting in a flat deck contour. A shaper may utilize a thin, tapered rail that is easier (especially for a smaller, lighter surfer) to sink and lean on edge. A shaper may concentrate or increase the amount of foam down the stringer (midline) of the board to maintain or improve flotation when a thin, tapered rail is required for control. This is typically utilized on gun boards, as a thicker stringer is more resistant to breakage. A rail that is thin in relation to the stringer thickness results in a domed deck contour as the thickness smoothly tapers from the thicker stringer to the thinner rail. Deck contours influence the way a board feels when you pick it up, paddle it and ride it. Note the types of deck contours you've grown accustomed to and keep that in mind when evaluating a new shape.

Bottom Contours - 90° to the Stringer

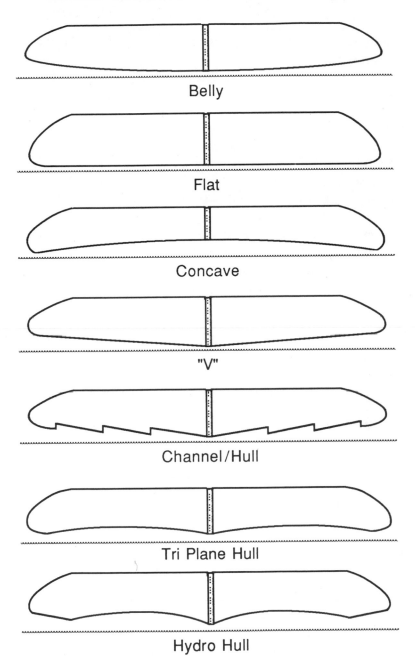

Belly

Flat

Concave

"V"

Channel/Hull

Tri Plane Hull

Hydro Hull

Bottom Contours–90° to the Stringer

Belly: a convex planing surface
Flat: a flat planing surface
Concave: a concave planing surface
"V":   a faceted planing surface
Channel/Hull: a series of flat/concave planes
Tri Plane Hull: a double concave planing surface
Hydro Hull: a double concave planing surface with increased "V" and a dual edged rail

Note: *Most boards are made with a combination of bottom contours.*

Belly–A convex planing surface is the most inefficient. The convex curve plows through the water and parts it, allowing it to escape off the rail. Belly is usually used as an aid to control. It will give a smoother ride in choppy conditions because rather than slapping against the water it will part it. In big or fast surf belly allows the surfboard to roll or lean from rail to rail easier, which is essential for control at high speeds.

Flat–Flat bottoms plane up on top of the water making them efficient and responsive. They are quick and loose in small or mushy surf. Once higher speeds are reached, flat bottoms are a bit more difficult to initiate turns with, and tend to skitter or slide when turned hard.

Concave–The purpose of a concave bottom is to contain water flow down the length of the board. The water under the wide point is necked down and squeezed out in the tail area which brings the venturi principle into play, resulting in more lift. The addition of concaves can either remove or add rocker depending on their placement. Rocker must be adjusted accordingly so that desired performance characteristics are maintained. Concaves are a potent design feature and can cause a board to track and feel stiff to delicate adjustment in line if utilized improperly.

"V"–Angled "V" on the bottom works very much like belly, but is a flat plane rather than a convex curve. Usually belly is found on the forward $1/3$ of the board and "V" is found on the rear $2/3$. "V" is essential to loosen up the tail area at high speeds. "V" increases the rocker at the rail line which makes the board turn more easily. Many surfers experience a feeling of added projection out of turns on boards with pronounced "V", which may be attributed to the "V" allowing them to turn harder, with the flat planes maintaining an efficient planing surface. Increased "V" makes a board easier to lean.

Channel/Hull Bottom–The channel bottom consists of a series of flat planes (usually 2-8 in number) that are angled in a concave configuration. The main advantage to this design is that it directs waterflow down the length of the channel. Since the channels are parallel, the water isn't being compressed as it is in the full concave. The channel bottom design provides the advantages of a full concave without the disadvantages of being stiff or tracking. The concave configurations of these planes contain and direct water down their length when a turn is made instead of letting water escape off the rail. More of the energy put into the turn is utilized and converted to forward thrust. As a rule, longer and deeper channels give maximum effect while short and shallow channels are more subtle.

Special attention should be paid to the corners of the channels to make sure they are benefitting from a full strength glass job.

Tri Plane Hull–The tri plane hull was developed by Al Merrick and consists of a shallow concave on each side of the stringer that extends from the center of the board to the fin(s). Added lift is created as water passes diagonally across this contour; similar in action to water rushing over a stone in a stream. The effect of the tri plane hull is similar to channels but more subtle. Channels have more directional sense, producing more drive and projection out of turns, but the tri plane hull is quicker in leaning edge to edge.

Hydro Hull–The hydro hull adds a double edged rail and subtle double concaves to a bottom with increased "V". The beveled rail facilitates release yet maintains a nose to tail edge for bite and projection. The forward ¾ of the rail is the widest point of the hydro rail. This is also where the subtle double concaves start. The double concaves create lift (improving planing efficiency) and remove rocker curve which creates a straighter, faster rocker. The improved planing efficiency of this design allows narrower template dimensions to be utilized. Decreased width coupled with increased "V" improve quick response in rail to rail transitions.

Effects of Bottom Contours on Rocker

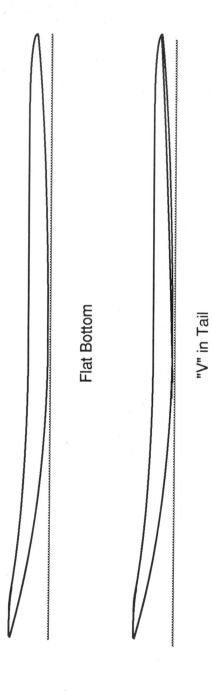

Flat Bottom

"V" in Tail

Effects of Bottom Contours on Rocker

If a board were shaped with a perfectly flat bottom from nose to tail, the rocker curve down the middle of the board and at the rail would be the same, but this is rarely the case. The addition of bottom contours creates two rocker curves – one down the middle and one at the rail of the board. Concaves decrease the rocker in the middle of the board in relation to the rail. Belly (used in the nose) and "V" (used in the middle or tail) increases the rocker curve at the rail in relation to the rocker down the middle of the board.

Tail Designs

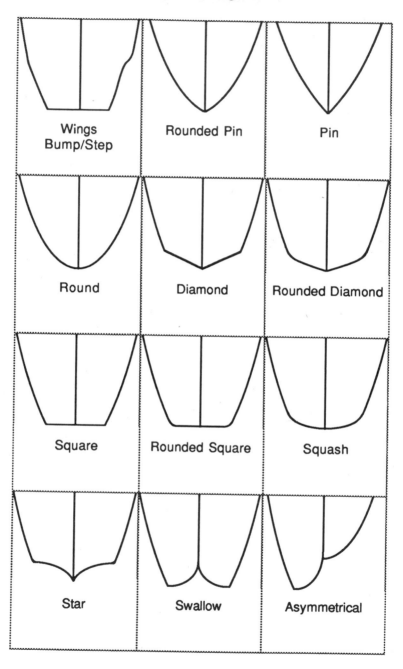

Wings Bump/Step

Rounded Pin

Pin

Round

Diamond

Rounded Diamond

Square

Rounded Square

Squash

Star

Swallow

Asymmetrical

Tail Designs

Almost any tail design can be blended into any template. Many of the designs have very subtle influences on performance. When looking at tail shapes, remember that curves hold water flow whereas corners allow water flow to break away. The tail width is usually a more accurate indication of board performance than the tail design.

The narrower and more pointed tail designs have a longer, more drawn out turning characteristic and are oriented for faster, larger surf. The minimal planing area is essential to control at high speeds but causes sluggish response, drags, and turns poorly in small or slow surf.

A wide, full tail has a great deal of planing area which suits it to small and slow surf. Greater tail area aids in paddling, planing, flotation, and wave catching ability. Wide tails will do sharp pivotal turns with very little projection. They are very loose because their great planing area keeps them from sinking and dragging.

Multi-fin systems are utilized to keep wide tails from spinning out. Wide points have moved back and tail widths have been proportionally increased as multi-fin systems have proven their ability to maintain control. Increased tail area and multi-fin systems have helped create equipment that is fast, loose and positive. Wide tails are an advantage in small or slow surf because their increased width improves planing efficiency. A variety of multi-fin systems are utilized for smaller surf, with the tri fin a strong favorite. For larger surf the superiority of the tri fin is unrivaled – though debate persists on the advantages of tri vs. single fin on narrow tailed Waimea guns.

Wings/Bump Wings/Stingers (not shown)–Wings, bump wings, and stingers are shifts in the template that alter the rail line. They vary in placement, as well as in how pronounced they are. The shaper can use them with any rail design to set up a break/pivot point in the rail line that will loosen the board's turning characteristic.

Wings are small, pronounced (almost 90°) shifts in the rail line that are typically placed anywhere from 3"-15" from the tip of the tail. One, two, or three pairs of wings can be used with any tail design to enhance maneuverability. Wings allow shapers to utilize the looser turning characteristic of the wider tail ahead of the wings with the holding power of the narrower tail immediately following them. Wings break/shorten the length of the rail line which makes the board looser. Wings are rarely utilized on boards for larger waves because they create a point in the rail where water breaks away, which compromises control at higher speeds. Bump wings are smoother and more subtle than wings. They appear as slight bumps or exaggerated transitions in the template curve. Bump wings are designed to maintain water flow along the rail so that the water bends into a narrower tail rather than breaking away. Stingers resemble pronounced wings that are placed approximately $1/3$ (the board length) up from the tip of the tail; where they act as a pivot point between the front and rear foot. Stingers break/shorten the length of the rail line to create a looser more pivotal turning characteristic. Like wings, the use of stingers is typically limited to boards designed for smaller surf, where the increased looseness they provide won't compromise control.

Rounded Pin Tail – The standard. This is the tail by which all others are judged. The rounded pin is a very versatile tail. It is very smooth in rail to rail transitions and holds-in well.

Pin Tail – The big wave, full race version of the rounded pin. Pin tails have a minimum amount of area. This is why they hold-in well at high speeds in big surf. A no-compromise solution to control at the higher speeds common to large surf.

Round Tail – A very smooth turning tail that has a bit more area than the rounded pin. The extra area makes it more suitable for slower, smaller surf.

Diamond Tail – The corners of the diamond tail make its turning characteristics a bit more pivotal and sharper than the rounded pin.

Rounded Diamond Tail – A diamond tail with rounded corners that is very similar to a rounded pintail or round tail in design and performance.

Square Tail – The square tail contains the greatest area of any tail design. The square tail design will carve the sharpest, most pivotal turns and be most responsive.

Rounded Square Tail – The rounded square tail is a subdued version of the square tail. It is somewhat less responsive. The turn it carves is not quite as sharp and pivotal because of its rounded corners.

Squash Tail – The squash tail is very similar in appearance to the rounded square tail – performance will be very similar.

Star Tail – The star tail is very similar to a diamond tail except for the reverse curves leading to the accentuated point. Its performance is similar to a diamond tail with a bit more projection out of turns, and a bit more ease in turning at higher speeds. The star tail can be considered a combination of a diamond or square tail and pintail.

Swallow Tail – The swallow tail is basically two pin tails side by side. The swallow tail design couples substantial tail area with the control of a pintail. The area it contains is very close to a square tail but the individual pins hold in much better when the board is turned hard.

The only problem with swallow tails is that in radical changes of direction the tip of one side must be disengaged totally before the tail will pivot freely on the other pin. This makes for a tail that tracks or is somewhat stiff in transitions from rail to rail. The swallow tail will feel totally positive when banked and committed, but when direction and rail is to be switched, a hesitation in the transition from one pin to the other can be noticed.

Asymmetrical Tail – Most surfers draw different lines when surfing backside than they do frontside. Their frontside style may be more driving and down the line. At the same time their backside style or the wave they usually surf backside may demand a more vertical up and down attack with lots of cutbacks. The asymmetrical tail allows the surfer to choose the type of tail most suited to his front and back side styles and the types of waves he rides most often.

Fins

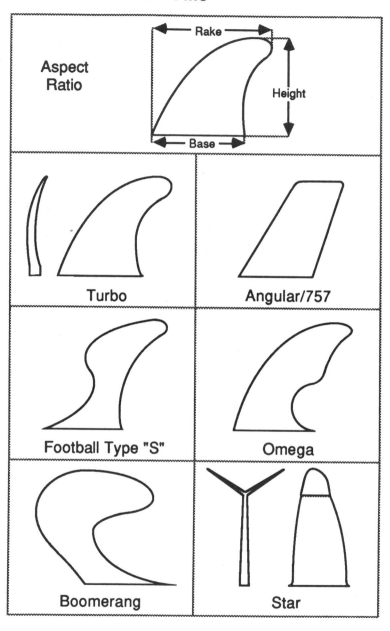

Aspect
Ratio

Rake

Height

Base

Turbo

Angular/757

Football Type "S"

Omega

Boomerang

Star

◀ **Direction of Travel/Nose of Board** ━━

Fins

The finest shape is useless without a fin. Just as a shape can be designed to suit particular needs, fins can also be selected for their effect on performance. Usually the more area a fin has the better it will hold in. The trade off is a stiffer turning characteristic. The way the fin area is arranged determines how the fin will influence the performance of the shape.

The more tail area a board possesses, the more fin area it's going to need to hold it in. The requirements of fin area can be met by having one large fin or two, three or four smaller fins.

Base and height describe the area of the fin, while rake describes the way the fin area is arranged.

Base - The distance between the leading and trailing edges of the fin, where the fin meets the board.

Height - The distance from the bottom of the board to the top of the fin.

More Height/Wider Base - increased area, slightly stiffer turning initiation, more holding in potential.

Less Height/Narrower Base - decreased area, easier to turn, less potential to hold in, tendency to drift or slide.

To keep your board as loose as possible, use the smallest fin(s) that will provide the control you need. As boards go longer and tails get narrower as in the case of guns, fins should be reduced in size as well as moved up to maintain looseness.

Experimentation with windsurfers has shown that water flowing down the length of the board interferes with water flow around the base of the fin, creating turbulence around the base. Shortening the base minimizes this effect, creating a fin that exhibits a looser turning characteristic. The reduced base area is actually more efficient as waterflow was parting off the longer base. The reduced base area is looser rail to rail and in sharp pivot turns yet holds in just as well when the board is leaned on edge because area at the tip is maintained.

Rake - Rake refers to the angle or attitude the leading edge of the fin has in relation to its base. Rake describes the way fin area is arranged in relation to the base, which indicates the way the fin will influence performance.

More Rake - a more drawn out (longer) turning radius.

Less Rake - a sharper, more pivotal (shorter) turning radius.

Forward Rake – The leading edge of the fin extends ahead of its base which utilizes a wider looser tail area and places the holding power of the fin closer to your rear foot.

Vertical Rake – The leading edge of the fin extends straight up, with the fin area centered directly over the base. This type of rake provides the most pivotal turning characteristic for it influences the water for the shortest distance.

Rearward Rake – The leading edge of the fin sweeps back, extending behind its base which utilizes a narrower, more positive tail area and results in a longer more drawn out turning characteristic.

Fin Placement – A fin box allows you to adapt your board to a variety of wave sizes. Moving the fin forward in the box lets you utilize a wider looser tail for small waves. This will create a sharper, more pivotal turning characteristic. Moving the fin up too far will cause the board to drift, slide and exhibit poor projection out of turns. Moving the fin back in the box utilizes a narrower tail for better control in larger waves and at higher speeds. With the fin moved back the turns will be longer and more drawn out.

Multi-Fin Placement – The fins on multi-fin designs are positioned then set at particular angles to maximize performance. The angles are referred to as toe in and cant. The proximity of the fin to the rail also influences the turning characteristics of a multi-fin. When the fins are closer to the rail (further apart) the board will hold in better, get more projection out of turns, and exhibit a stiffer turning characteristic. Setting the fins further from the rail (closer together) will result in a looser, more pivotal turning characteristic that won't hold in as well and will result in decreased projection out of turns.

The way a multi-fin cluster is grouped influences performance in a similar fashion. The tighter the cluster is grouped (with front and rear fins closer together) the more pivotal the turning characteristic. More distance between front and rear fins causes a more drawn out turning characteristic.

Moving the fin cluster forward as a complete set utilizes a wider tail area which results in a looser more pivotal turning characteristic. Moving the cluster back utilizes a narrower tail area which holds in better and provides a more drawn out turning characteristic. The fin cluster is usually moved up on longer gun boards so it's easier to turn the board when you're standing further forward.

Toe In and Camber

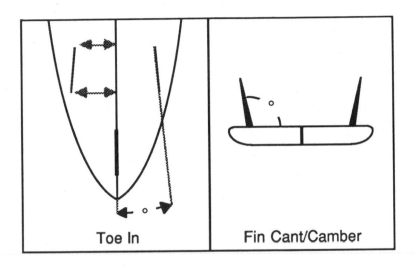

Toe In   Fin Cant/Camber

Fin Toe In – Increasing the toe in (the angle toward the stringer) makes the board looser by allowing it to turn tighter arcs. Increased toe in enlarges the apparent fin frontal area which increases drag and slows the board down. Decreasing the toe in (straightening the fins so they are more parallel to the stinger) creates a longer more drawn out turning characteristic and if taken to extremes will cause the board to track. Decreased toe in minimizes the apparent fin frontal area which minimizes drag and improves speed.

Fin Cant/Camber – Increasing the amount the fins are canted out (leaned away from the stringer), will result in a looser board with less drive and projection out of turns. At higher speeds, fins set-up with excessive cant will act like a hydrofoil and push the tail up. Decreasing the amount the fins are canted out creates a stiffer turning characteristic that results in more drive and projection out of turns.

Specialty Fins – Specialty fins are an inexpensive way to fine tune the performance of your board. With several fins you can increase the size range that your board will work in making it more versatile. If you are interested in perfecting a particular maneuver, you can choose the type(s) of fin(s) that tune(s) your board to your style. Glen DeWitt, owner of Rainbow Fins, offers some information that should help you choose the most appropriate shape.

Turbo Fins – Turbo fins are curved through their height. This curve works together with the angled fin placement to create a subtle venturi effect and provides more drive and projection out of turns, especially on very lined up waves.

Angular 757 – Curves hold onto water flow where as straight edges and corners cause water to break away cleanly. Straight edges free the fin to pivot and turn with less drag than a fin designed with curves.

Football Type S/Omega/Boomerang – These fin designs have been borrowed from high performance windsurfers. The narrow base makes it easier to lean the board rail to rail. The tip area is maintained or increased so there's plenty of fin in the water when the board is leaned on edge. These fins will resist sliding and spinning out in critical situations. The Omega design is the least likely to grab kelp, etc. as it passes through the water.

Star Fin – The star fin was conceived by Cheyn Horan and designed by Ben Lexcen. It's vertically oriented rake creates a snappy, pivotal turning characteristic. The wings at the tip improve drive and projection but have a tendency to lock the board into particular attitudes that cause a slight hesitation to delicate adjustments.

Glass-on Fins – Glass-on fins afford slightly cleaner water flow than the fin box as well as a savings in weight. The disadvantages of glass-on fins are that they can't be moved and they discourage experimentation with different fin designs. Also, glass-on fins are more susceptible to damage during travel.

True Foil – Foil is the cross section of the fin 90 degrees to its height. The curve should be symmetrical. The true foil keeps the water from breaking away from it for its entire length. A poor foil allows water to break away and the ensuing eddys and turbulence cause vibration and hum. The closer the fin comes to having a true foil, the easier it will pivot in the water.

Fin Foil Cross Sections

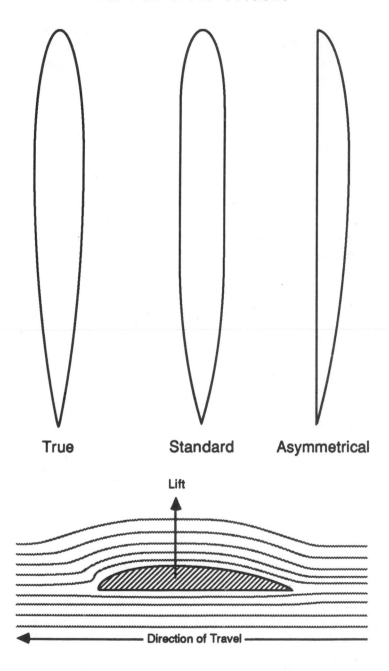

True Standard Asymmetrical

Lift

Direction of Travel

Standard Foil – The standard foil comes about as the result of the fin manufacturing process. Sheets of fiberglass are laminated, sometimes with layers of different colors. The sheets are made flat and to fit the thickness of a finbox. The desired fin template is cut out of the sheet. Then, the edges of the fin are tapered, or foiled, with a sander. The fin is finished with gloss resin, and polished. Building up additional layers of fiberglass to provide enough thickness so that the continuous curve of a true foil could be accommodated, and then removing the excess material so that the fin would still fit in the box, would add expense, weight, and probably would go unnoticed by most surfers. For this reason, the most reasonably priced fins with true foils are cast in plastic.

Asymmetrical Foil – Most twin and tri-fin side fins are foiled only on the outside edge. The inside edge of these fins is straight. Surfaces that are foiled on one side have the potential of producing lift. Lift is created when flow is faster across one side of a structure than another. When the fin passes through the water at a particular speed, the velocity across the curved side of the foil is faster than it is across the flat side of the foil. The side which has the faster velocity across it has lower pressure upon it. This imbalance of pressure creates lift. The asymmetrically foiled fins are set so that the straight sides are toward the center of the board. The lift created by the asymmetrical foil pulls the fin into the face of the wave.

Fin Modifications – Fins can be changed in shape. If you can't find the type of fin(s) you think your board needs, you can cut down and refoil a larger fin or build up a smaller fin with resin and glass.

Foam fins are occasionally used as people start looking closely at construction details for savings in weight. The recent move to very thin fins on multi-fin boards to reduce fin frontal area and drag, reduces the benefits of this technique. I have personally used foam fins that were shaped and foiled from higher density foam, then glassed with five layers of four ounce cloth. A bead of glass rope was used at the leading edge of the fin for additional impact resistance. The fins weighed six to seven ounces, were light and durable.

Another technique to save weight is to cut the center of the fin out, and replace this area with a piece of foam, then refoil and reglass the foam into place. This gives you a tough fiberglass edge to resist damage, with a foam core to save weight.

Flexible Fins–The idea behind the flexible fin is to store and release turning energy at the time most opportune to performance. As a turn is initiated, the fin flexes absorbing and storing the energy. As the turning pressure is released, the fin snaps back into line, releasing the stored energy and providing additional forward thrust. Plastic fins or fins set up with epoxy resin rather than polyester resin usually have a superior resiliency or memory for use in this application. Horizontal cuts starting from the trailing edge of the fin and leading up to within one or two inches of the leading edge also influence flex. The cuts can be made with a hacksaw and are usually one half inch away from the base and stacked evenly one half inch apart to the tip of the fin.

It is important to realize that not all turns required in surfing are of the "hit it hard then release" variety. Sometimes long, drawn out turns are required on long sections or to get around whitewater. Very subtle adjustments in line may also be necessary. Subtle turns may flex the fin without actually influencing the direction of the board. Since the fin creates a turn from leaning input, a flexible fin is going to distort that relationship. Expect delayed response in turn initiation and then an added thrust coming out of the turn. These delayed reactions may throw your timing off or they may enhance your surfing.

Fin Hum–Fin hum is usually created by a distrubance of water flow off the top two or three inches of the fin. The disturbed water flow sets up a vibration in the tip of the fin that we detect as hum when riding the board. An imperfect foil two or three inches from the tip is most often the cause of fin hum. Make sure the thickness of the foil tapers near the tip so the water doesn't go through too many changes too fast. Water is likely to break away from the foil if it encounters a thin leading edge, a thick center section foil and a thin trailing edge in too short a distance. A blunt or flat trailing edge will cause water to break away rather than releasing cleanly. Sharply foiled trailing edges don't hum but are obviously dangerous. The best compromise for clean release and safety is attained by chamfering (beveling) the rear edge of the fin. To do this, foil the trailing edge sharp, then for safety go back over the sharp edge with a 45° chamfer. On asymmetrically foiled fins, the chamfer should start on the foiled side and end on the flat side. On standard foils, the chamfer can start or end on either side. Turbulence and resulting hum is created when water flows off a blunt trailing edge. The chamfering technique allows water to taper cleanly off the fin providing the benefits of a sharp trailing edge without compromising safety.

Cavitation – Cavitation typically occurs at higher speeds in combination with increased turning loads. Cavitation is a disruption of the water flow around a fin that occurs when the water pressure surrounding the fin isn't high enough to force the water pushed aside by the leading edge back into contact with the rest of the fin. This leaves a vapor filled cavity next to the fin – disrupting flow and control. An abrupt or pivotal turn at higher speeds may induce cavitation and break a fin loose causing it to drift, slide, or spin out. Chop, bump or froth on the face of a wave create variance in the water pressure surrounding the fin, making cavitation (and loss of control) much more likely to occur. Fin hum (indicating disruption in water flow) may hint at a predisposition to cavitation, however many fins that suffer from cavitation in isolated instances never hum. George Downing has designed a "Bong" fin, with a specialized template and a foiled torpedo tip that he feels helps prevent cavitation. Sailboarders utilize single fins to keep fin frontal area (and drag) to a minimum. They use a small, foiled fore fin placed just ahead of the leading edge of the fin. The fore fin directs waterflow in a manner that minimizes the occurance of cavitation.

Custom Surfboards

When your ideas about surfboard design have become so focused that you know exactly what you want but you can't find it in any shop's stock, it's time for a custom. Not every shaper has the ability to shape anything you want, so pick the shaper that comes the closest to creating the design you want in his stock boards. Talk directly to the shaper or his closest associate at the shop. If there is great distance involved and traveling is inconvenient, send a letter along with your order that specifies everything that is essential to your being satisfied with the board.

When ordering a custom surfboard it is essential that you provide the shaper with as much accurate and detailed information as possible. Keep records of all important design measurements of your boards. If you've ridden a friend's board and really liked or disliked it, measure it. Note what types of waves the board worked best in, what kinds of maneuvers it excelled at and whether the board worked best backside or frontside. This will give you insight into design directions you should pursue or avoid. Note specific bottom, rail, and thickness contours. Make sure all your measurements are accurate, because rocker and template curves have a dimensional progression that will be upset and confused by inaccurate measurements.

Make sure to describe the types of waves you want the board to work in. Think about the spot you surf the most and its average size. It makes sense to tailor the board to the waves you ride most often, rather than altering the design for those few days per year that the waves take on a different character. If you enjoy taking surf trips to a spot that has a much different wave than you normally surf, don't try to make a compromise board that will not perform well at either spot. Instead, have two boards made, each tailored to your exact needs for each spot. Your boards will work well, and you'll have the confidence that you are on the best equipment possible enabling you to surf better and enjoy yourself more.

Inform the shaper of your height and weight. Your weight will determine the thickness of your board and influence its width. If you are quite tall and have large feet you may require a wider tail to keep your rear foot from dragging through the water during hard turns and because you can produce more leaning/turning force.

I have been fortunate in dealing with Mike Eaton for my personal boards. He has over thirty years of experience and has shaped over

25,000 surfboards. Mike has devoted his life to experimenting with surfboards, sailboats, and sailplanes. Since aero and hydro dynamics are closely related, he has developed a very thorough practical expertise about design. He is also a superb craftsman. When he shapes, he is like a man possessed – running back and forth about the blank, not wasting a motion. He seems to have a perfect picture in his mind of what the finished blank will look like. He uses his planer and sander to remove excess foam quickly and surely transforming the rough exterior into dust and leaving only a clean flowing design on the racks.

Mike has shaped everything from five foot kneeboards to twelve foot Waimea guns. Over the years he has satisfied some of the world's most dynamic surfers during the peaks of their careers. Through all this he has retained boundless enthusiasm and has remained very approachable. His world travels qualify him to shape boards for exotic breaks with first hand experience. It takes Mike about 40 minutes to shape a board. If you are watching him create your personal design, he will stop at critical facets of the process and motion you into the shaping room to evaluate the progress. He won't push his ideas on you but will call on his immense store of experience to create the type of board you want.

My association with SURFER Magazine has compelled me to work with many different shapers trying out different approaches to design. Charley Baldwin, Brian Bulkley, Matt Kechele, Al Merrick, Steve Morgan, Rusty Preisendorfer, Robin Prodanovich and Bill Stewart are some of the shapers that have stoked me with their boards. In most cases I rarely specify more than length, width and thickness so I can try their idea of a good board. I've been consistently impressed with the performance routinely built into todays equipment by top shapers . Many top shapers rely on feeback from pro surfers and team riders to refine their equipment. It is essential that those interested in customized equipment understand design so they can improve rather than undermine their chances for a better board.

Surfboard Construction Materials

Blank – Polyester based urethane foam blanks are shaped into various designs.

Fiberglass Cloth – Glass fibers that are woven into a cloth. Weights of 4 oz., 6 oz., etc., refer to the weight of a square yard of cloth. Lighter cloths are finer and weaker. Heavier cloths are coarser and stronger.

Polyester Resin/Catalyst – Various resins are used in the construction of the surfboard. They must be mixed with a particular proportion of catalyst in order to harden. The more catalyst used, the faster it will harden. Use too much or too little and it won't harden at all. Warmer temperatures cause resin to harden faster, while cooler temperatures inhibit the hardening process. Amounts of catalyst must be adjusted accordingly.

Laminating Resin – The base resin. Various agents are added to this resin to make it suitable for other processes. Laminating resin is used in applying the fiberglass cloth to the shaped blank. This resin stays tacky and is unsandable.

Sanding or Surfacing Resin – These resins are used to fill in the texture and lap seams in the cloth. This resin has a surfacing agent (a wax which floats to the surface once the resin is applied, blocking air from the resin) added to it that causes it to set up hard and tack free. The sanding resin is sanded to make the board smooth.

Gloss Resin – This resin is thinned and has leveling and surfacing agents added to it. Gloss resin is the final coat of resin applied to the surfboard. The gloss coat is wet sanded and polished to give the board its smooth, glossy finish.

Styrene – A resin thinner. If you have a shatter on your board that you would like to get rid of, sand down to the cloth, and apply styrene. The styrene will saturate around the glass fibers and make the shatter disappear. Build the sand and gloss coats up again, polish the area out, and it will look like new.

Acetone – The solvent most commonly used to dissolve catalized or uncatalized resin.

Surfboard Construction Materials
and Your Health

Some of the materials used in surfboard construction are quite toxic and can cause health problems if used carelessly. When working with foam or sanding dust, use a respirator with a dust catching pre-filter. The most commonly used cheap white dust masks are virtually ineffective in protecting your lungs. Particles large enough to see are filtered by the hairs in your nose or land on the mucous membranes of your throat. The particles can then get blown out of your nose or swallowed, where they pass through your digestive system without bothering your lungs. The invisible particles pose the greatest threat to lungs and only a sophisticated respirator can filter them.

Fiberglass can irritate your skin and cause you to itch. Gel facial mask applied to skin irritated by tiny glass fibers will pull the fibers out once it has dried and is peeled off.

Resin fumes can irritate the respiratory tract and cause headaches, nausea and dizzyness. Styrene, an ingredient and thinner of resin can irritate the eyes, nose, throat and skin. Roughly ten percent of the styrene present in resin evaporates during the curing process. Since resin is almost half styrene, a lot of stryene ends up in the air you may be breathing. Styrene is also absorbed through the skin.

Catalyst is roughly sixty percent methyl ethyl ketone peroxide. MEKP is extremely irritating to the skin, eyes and respiratory tract. Don't breath it, get it on your skin, or in your eyes. If you do get some on your skin, immediately wash it off with soap and water. If you get it in your eyes, rinse them for at least fifteen minutes with room temperature water. If eye effects persist, see a doctor as soon as possible.

Acetone can cause eye, nose and throat irritation. When acetone is inhaled, approximately 75% is absorbed into the bloodstream. It takes three to five days for your system to eliminate it. Acetone damages skin by removing natural oils and is absorbed through the skin as well.

One last caution; if you're ever around a burning surfboard, make sure nobody inhales any of the smoke. It is highly toxic, containing traces of hydrogen cyanide, the chemical used in gas chambers.

If you plan on working with these materials invest in your health and buy a good respirator. Binks, De Vilbiss and Survivair are the best I've used and they all come with replaceable cartridges. Use organic vapor cartridges for dealing with fumes and particulate filters for dust.

Use gloves to protect your skin and prevent chemicals from being absorbed through your skin. Wear eye protection when working with catalyst. Work in a well ventilated area and take care that others aren't inadvertently exposed to the fumes and dust you create. If you need additional information contact the Surfer's Medical Association, 2396 Great Highway / 48th Ave., S.F., Calif. 94116 (415) 664-7027.

Tools Used in Surfboard Construction

Respirator – A respirator is a mask that filters the air you breathe. Some of the materials and processes used in surfboard construction can expose you to unhealthy fumes and dust. Cheap masks don't protect you from these toxic substances. High quality respirators, such as the ones made by Binks, De Vilbiss, and Survivair are available from paint spraying companies. The respirators should be equipped with organic vapor cartridges for working with resin fumes. You can extend the useful life of these filter cartridges (which contain activated charcoal) by storing your respirator in a clean, airtight container or ziplock bag. Particulate pre-filters remove dust and particulate matter. Respirators are routinely used by concientious craftsmen in the industry. They cost about thirty dollars, have renewable filters and are a great investment in your health.

Planer – Hand-held power planers are used by shapers to quickly and accurately remove foam from blanks. The planers were created for working on wood, and take foam down instantly. Professional shapers create the majority of the shape with a power plane. Power planers take foam down so quickly that mistakes in handling them can be disastrous.

Sander – The power sander is used by the shaper to smooth out ridges left by the planer, and by the sander to sand the surfboard smooth.

Surform – A surform is a rasp-like plane with removable blades. It is used on foam and glass/resin.

Screen/Grit Cloth – This is a screen-like cloth with abrasive particles bonded to it. Grit cloth is used on foam to blend rail contours. It allows particles to pass through it so it doesn't clog up like sandpaper.

Sandpaper – Abrasives used from 50-600 grit.

Router – A high speed router is used to install leash cups and finboxes. The high rpm and power of this tool allows for very precise and clean penetration of foam and fiberglass.

Blank Specification Sheet

6'5"P

USE: Medium board

HISTORY: #1 seller·

REPLACEMENTS: 6'5", 6'5"B, 6'6"B, 7'5".

ROCKERS: Natural, +1/2"N, +1"N, Rawson

LIMITED VOLUME CHARGE: None

FACTORY STOCKING: Always

SPECIAL: Blown out of 7'5" mold. Universally accepted.

NOTE: Actual length 6'7"

ACTUAL LENGTH 6'7"

←—3¼"

←—5⅜"

←—15⅛"

38½"

←—2¼"

6'-7"

←—22"

←—3⁵⁄₁₆"

←—18⁵⁄₁₆

←—2¹¹⁄₁₆"

CUBE: 2.230 cu. ft.
.063 M3

←—14"→

→←—1⅝"

SHAPED BY TOM PARRISH

CLARK FOAM

Materials and Techniques Used In
Surfboard Construction

Almost everyone who touches your surfboard as it evolves from the glimmer in a shaper's eye to the board you got the waves of your life on, has to be a craftsman. Every stage is critical and must be done correctly to create a board of the highest quality.

The Blank – Gordon Clark developed and refined the process of creating polyurethane blanks from which surfboards are shaped. Clark Foam blows blanks in nearly fifty different lengths and rocker configurations. Shapers have dimensional information (length, width, rocker configurations, thickness flow) on every blank Clark has. The shaper can pick the blank that is most suitable for the type of board he wishes to create. The shaper also has the option of having the rocker in the blank altered and glued up to his specification. Many of the world's top shapers have designed blanks which facilitate them in the execution of their designs.

The blank is strongest near its outside layer or skin because that's where the foam cells are the most dense. The closer the dimensions of the blank are to the finished shape, the stronger the blank remains, resulting in a stronger board. Blanks come in superlight, supergreen (8% lighter than superlight), superblue (12½% lighter than superlight) and ultralight (25% lighter than superlight) densities. The lighter blanks are also the weaker blanks.

New blanks are designed by top contemporary shapers that find they are removing too much foam or consistently modifying rocker when using existing blanks to shape their latest designs. The original design of a blank (called a plug) is shaped and glassed by the shaper that feels there is a need for the new design. The plug is often carried on rounds by Clark's delivery truck, so other shapers have a chance to evaluate the design. If there is sufficient interest, Clark puts the design into production. The first step is to make a cement mold of the plug. The cement is six to twelve inches larger than the blank in all dimensions. The mold is cast with threaded steel inserts in place so that it can be bolted into steel hydraulic arms when a run of the particular blank is needed. The blanks are blown in a room that is temperature and humidity controlled. Blanks are blown around the clock. The chemicals that are poured are so toxic that the atmosphere of the room is constantly monitored. The mold is preheated to a specific temperature essential to the foam producing chemicals. Once the mold is preheated and bolted into hydraulic arms, paper is laid down the length of its interior and the combination of chemicals is poured in. The thick white liquid undergoes a chemical reaction creating foam. The cement molds contain the expansion to achieve the desired dimensions. The temperature and pour are essential to consistent foam cell density. After 23 to 25 minutes the cement mold is opened and the blank, totally covered with paper, is removed. After laying on the floor for a while to set, the paper is removed. Then the blank is labelled and laid above a set of long fluorescent lights to be examined. Any voids are discovered, and the blank is classified as either a first, second, or a reject.

The blanks are then transferred to another section of the plant where they are cut for stringers or glue lines. Once cut, the surfaces are brushed with glue, the stringer is set into place, and hydraulic arms clamp the components into place. The glue sets for half an hour, and any excess stringer is taken down. At this point the blank is ready for shaping.

Stringer - The stringer is a long strip of wood glued into the blank to provide longitudinal strength. The stringer keeps the deck and bottom fiberglass skins equidistant thus acting as an "I beam" type stiffener. The stringer is usually one-sixteenth to one-quarter of an inch wide and is unbroken through the full length and thickness of the blank. Stringers make the board more resistant to snapping in half, flexing, and vibrating from slapping chop. The longer or thinner the board is, the more important the properties of the stringer become. Sometimes more than one stringer is used for increased strength or aesthetic preference.

Various woods are used for stringers, including redwood, balsa, basswood, butternut and spruce. Qualities of the wood, including flexibility, weight, and strength, influence the thickness used. Properties of various woods are matched to the blank depending on probable uses. Adding thickness to a board increases its stiffness and resistance to breakage much more than increasing the width of the stringer or varying the type of wood it is made of.

Clark will also glue up custom stringers. Various woods available on a limited basis, as well as combinations of different stringers, can be requested. Additional stringers are called offsets because they are usually placed several inches on either side of the center stringer.

Paper stringers and colored glue lines are also used occassionally.

Shaping–The shaper picks the blank most suitable to his needs. Dimensions are plotted on the bottom and a template curve is used to connect the points. To get the smoothest, most flowing line for a set of custom dimensions a number of templates may be used. The drawn template is cut out with a hand or sabre saw. The rough outer skin of the blank is planed off and the bottom contours and rail radii are planed in. The board is flipped over, the deck is planed down to the desired thickness, and the rails are turned-down. All the planer ridges are smoothed down with a power sander. The rails, which are still faceted at this point, are blended into smooth curves with a surform and screen cloth. The stringer is taken down with a small hand plane, the blank is fine-sanded, fin positions are marked and the blank is signed. There is a great deal of attention paid to design idosyncracies unique to the shaper during the shaping process. The blending of necessary elements into a flowing design make shaping as much an art as a craft.

Laminating–After the blank is shaped it is covered with fiberglass cloth and resin. The surfboard industry utilizes cloth weights of four ounce, six ounce, and seven and one-half ounce, depending on the application. The lighter cloths are also thinner so additional weight is saved because they are saturated by a thinner, lighter layer of resin. The lighter cloths are also weaker. In the past, a typical production glass job would consist of a double layer of six ounce on the deck and a single layer of six ounce on the bottom, with a tail patch in the fin area. The increased demand for lighter equipment has resulted in several strategies. Most utilize a single layer of four ounce on the bottom (with or without a tail patch in the fin area). On the deck, a full length layer of six ounce used with a full length layer of four ounce is one alternative. Two full length layers of four ounce are also used quite often. Another option is a single full length layer of four ounce on the deck supplemented by two staggered deck patches. The deck patches are two thirds and one third the length of the board ending at the tip of the tail. This results in a competition weight glass job that puts one layer of four ounce near the nose, two under your knees and three under your rear foot (to act as a stomp patch). The deck always requires additional reinforcement to withstand repeated contact from knees and heels.

Gun boards are often glassed heavier because the extra weight lends them stability and helps them drive down the face through wind and chop. Guns are often reinforced with an additional three inch wide strip of cloth (narrower in the case of carbon fiber) over the stringer. This helps maintain the stringer's I-beam effect which increases stiffness and breaking strength.

The blank is set on the glassing stands and blown off with compressed air to remove any foam dust. The lap line is taped off, the cloth is laid down on the blank, and any wrinkles are smoothed out. The cloth is trimmed to the desired lap line and then nose and tail overlaps are cut. Acrylic paint may be airbrushed on the foam and the board glassed clear or a coloring agent may be mixed into the laminating resin. To color the resin, it is mixed with tint (transparent) or pigment (opaque), then strained. Silkscreened paper stickers are set into place with a bit of resin. The correct proportion of catalyst is mixed in, and the laminator pours the resin over the cloth, following the pour closely with a squeegee, which forces the resin into the cloth, thereby saturating it. If the laminator does not use enough resin the glass job is light, weak, dry, and interspersed with tiny air bubbles. If too much resin is used, the glass cloth floats in the resin, does not approximate the shaped blank as closely as possible, is excessively heavy and has impaired impact resistance. When the resin sets up, the laminated cloth is trimmed to the taped line with a razor.

The laminator can add: (1) extra tail patch of cloth in the fin area(s) for added strength–this helps to prevent cracks at the front of the finbox, or at the base of glass on fins; (2) deck patches–smaller areas of double-strength on the deck so that the reinforcement is placed exactly where you need it and weight is kept to a minimum; (3) stomp patches–a third layer of cloth in the tail area that strengthens the area beneath the rear foot (typically used on competition weight four ounce glass jobs); (4) split lap tails–the deck lamination is not lapped around the rear one foot of the tail rail, but left hanging, later to be trimmed and filled with the sanding coat to give an extra hard edge in the tail area. Fiberglass rope can be set into the freelap for extra strength. The tail area can also be lapped normally, with a resin bead added by taping off a small reservoir, filling it with resin and sanding it to the desired shape.

Volan cloth is usually used because it is easy to saturate and lap over. Sylene cloth which is a bit stiffer, is also used because it saturates with superior clarity and can be free-lapped. Free-lapping is the process of laying up a rail without trimming it. The cloth is just lapped over; no trimming, taping, or cutting. This technique is strongest because underlying layers of cloth aren't cut while trimming, but is not adaptable to all color designs.

Laminating

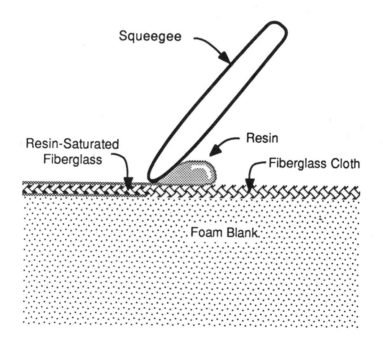

Surfacing/Sanding/Hot Coat - The sanding resin is laminating resin with a surfacing agent added to it. The surfacing agent is a wax which rises to the surface of the resin once it has been applied, and cuts off the air from the resin. The absence of air causes the resin to set up hard and tack-free, allowing it to be sanded.

After the blank is laminated, the peak (outermost edge) of the rail is taped-off and a coat of surfacing resin is brushed on. The laminating resin is formulated to stay tacky and never gets hard enough to sand. The sanding resin bonds to the tacky laminating resin and fills all the texture of the cloth. It also adds stiffness to the glassjob.

The deck of the surfboard is sandcoated, the tape is pulled off, and after the resin hardens, it is set bottom up on the racks. If fins are to be glassed on, suitable fins are chosen and the glasser locates the fins to the marks specified by the shaper. The fins are sanded thoroughly with 50-grit sandpaper and taped into position. Great care must be taken to make sure that the fins are positioned correctly. Once the fin is taped into position, the corner between the side of the fin and the bottom of the board is filled with saturated fiberglass rope. Then more cloth is added that lays up the side of the fin from the bottom of the board. Once the fins are reinforced sufficiently, the bottom is sandcoated.

If a finbox is to be used, the bottom is sandcoated and a channel for the box is cut out with a highspeed router. The fin channel on the box is taped up and the box is sanded. Laminating resin is used to saturate a piece of cloth that the box is wrapped in before it is set into it's trench. Leash cups are installed in the same manner, with a hole saw used to bore the hole rather than a router.

Now it's the sander's job to get the board totally smooth without sanding into the cloth and weakening the glass job. This requires a very experienced touch for: (1) the high speed sanders can sand through the cloth in an instant; (2) if the sander holds the machine over a single area for too long a time, even with a light touch, the cloth will overheat and delaminate from the blank. It is essential that the sander be familiar with the shaper's characteristics. The sander can enhance or destroy subtle elements that a shaper creates in a blank.

A sander usually has three machines. One machine is for grinding fin boxes and leash cups down, the second is equipped with a coarse sanding pad, and the third one is equipped with a fine sanding pad. Most of the board can be sanded by machine, but rails and corners at the base of glassed-on fins must be sanded by hand.

Pinstriping – Unless the board is glassed clear or a solid color, pinstripes are usually done on the lap lines. Both sides of the line are delineated with tape. The taping is very critical, for on long narrow lines deviations from a smooth curve become grossly apparent. Once the taping is finished, the line is applied with pigmented laminating resin or airbrushed acrylic, and the tape is pulled off.

Glossing – Once the color work has set up, glossing can begin. If sanding or gloss resin was used for the pinstripe, the stripe is lightly sanded to facilitate bonding of the gloss. The airbrushed acrylic goes on in such a thin layer, that bonding of the gloss resin to the originally sanded surface is hardly impaired. All the dust is removed, the peak of the rail is taped off, and the gloss resin is brushed on.

Gloss resin starts out as laminating resin. Then surfacing agent is added to it so that it will set up hard and tack free. Gloss resin is basically sanding resin with the addition of a resin thinner, styrene, and also the addition of a leveling agent. The styrene thins the gloss coat so it doesn't add much weight. The leveling agent is necessary to facilitate smoothing out after the gloss coat is brushed on. The gloss coat seals any glass fibers exposed during sanding, insuring the board is watertight.

Polishing – After the gloss resin has set up for at least twelve hours, it should be hard enough to polish. The seam where the deck and bottom gloss coats overlap on the peak of the rail is removed with a surform or file. Then the whole board is wet sanded with 320-, 400- and 600-grit papers successively. After wet sanding, the board is buffed out with abrasive rubbing and polishing compounds. Finally, a polish is applied and the board is ready for the customer.

Sanded Finishes – Competition boards are often finished with a fine sanded sand coat to save the weight of a gloss coat. The drawback to this finish is that the glass fibers left exposed after sanding tend to absorb water like a wick. Competitors spend a great deal of time in the water, push their surfing and equipment to the edge and frequently get new boards to keep pace with developing abilities. They move on to a new board before water absorbtion becomes a consequence. If you want a sanded finish, but plan on keeping your board for awhile, seal the finish with some sort of wax or consider a wet sanded gloss coat. The gloss seals the glass fibers, preventing water absorbtion. Some surfers feel that a sanded finish is a little faster and affords better grip than a polished finish. A bottom coating has been developed for sailboards called "Speedskin". The coating is applied to a fine sanded finish in two applications; primer and finish. "Speedskin" causes a thin layer of water to bond to the bottom once the board is wet. Once wet, the bottom of your board feels slick, like a wet catfish, (without the slimy residue), or the inside of your cheek. According to the manufacturer, this water on water lubrication results in a seventeen percent drag reduction. Benefits will mainly be apparent to competition caliber surfers that are very sensitive to equipment. The coating should be reapplied approximately every six months or whenever water beads up on the wet bottom. It softens when wet, and can be scuffed or scratched off. As it dries, it goes through a tacky stage (it was initially developed as a medical adhesive) at which time sand, towels, etc. will stick to it. Only use it if the performance benefits outweigh the extra effort required to take care of the bottom of your board.

Surfboard Weight vs Strength

A great deal of emphasis is put on the weight of surfboards. You may want the weight of a full strength glass job on a big wave gun. Common sense may dictate that you settle for the weight of a full strength glass job when you travel to some remote region where a damaged board may keep you out of the water. Or, you may prefer a feather weight that responds quickly in small slow surf.

The board should be as strong as possible for its weight. No dead weight, no unfunctional excesses in material that don't contribute to the strength of the board. The best way to get this type of board is to work with skillful, dedicated craftsmen.

Some details that can influence board weight and strength:

1. Make sure the board is shaped from the blank that comes closest to accommodating your conceived design. The shaper spends less time wasting foam and your finished shape is stronger because the foam cells closest to the exterior of the blank are more dense and stonger.

2. The amount of overlap on the rails can be changed to increase or decrease the amount of glass and strength on the rails.

3. Tailor deck patches to your needs – look at older boards and note where most of your deck dents normally occur. Have the deck patch trimmed to cover that area only. Make sure that deck patches are never cut straight across the stringer. This will create a line that makes your board more likely to snap at that point. Always have deck patches cut with as much angle as is practical.

4. If you are normally easy on the bottom of your board, have it done in four ounce rather than six ounce. The four ounce will decrease weight as well as strength.

5. You can request a textured deck. Textured decks are created by using a squeegee to apply the sanding resin instead of a brush. Weight savings result since less resin is applied initially and sanding/glossing steps are eliminated.

6. Clear glass jobs are usually a bit stronger per weight than tinted or pigmented counterparts. Streaks can result from heavy squeegee pressure on tinted boards so glassers sometimes leave them a bit wet for even color. A great deal of pigment must be added to the

resin to make it fully opaque and pigmenting agents as well as tinting agents have no strength. The resin is what you want in the glass–the coloring agents are dead weight. Acrylics are being sprayed on shaped blanks and sanded hot coats. This coloring system is extremely versatile, but the adhesion of the resin to the sprayed foam and sanded hot coat seems to be slightly impaired. The advantage to spraying a blank with acrylics before laminating, is that the blank is "sealed" so it absorbs less resin. Hot batches of resin can also save weight because they go off before soaking into the blank.

A thin board will flex more than a thick board with the same glass job. Increasing the thickness of a board (and its stringer) makes it stiffer and improves it's resistance to breakage. Before a board snaps, it flexes to its limit. If the forces flexing the board stop at this point you will typically find stress cracks running across (from rail to rail) the bottom. If the forces continue, the glass on one side is stretched tight and the glass on the other side is compressed. The glass that's being compressed starts to buckle up, delaminating from the foam. The board is weakened, flexing further as the delamination progresses until the glass on the other side is stretched so far that it finally tears apart. This is why broken boards often have a flap of delaminated glass hanging off one side and a clean break on the other.

Four ounce cloth has a tighter, finer weave that traps less resin than six ounce cloth and results in a superior strength to weight ratio. For this reason, three layers of four ounce would be stronger than two layers of six ounce. Careful sanding (i.e., the glass fibers aren't sanded into) makes the glass job as strong as possible.

Some people are using an aramid fiber cloth developed by Dupont called Kevlar instead of or in conjunction with fiberglass. The yellow aramid fiber is much more durable and lighter than the glass fiber. Kevlar has been used in the construction of bullet proof vests.

Carbon graphite fiber is extremely strong and light. Depending on the way it is incorporated into the design, it can be extremely rigid or allow continual flexibility without breakdown. It is also used in the construction of snow and waterskis, tennis racquets, jet fighters and Formula 1 racing car chassis. There is a six ounce fiberglass cloth that is reinforced with two strands of graphite every ½" on the warp (strands that run the length of the cloth–strands that run the width are referred to as welp or fill). Carbon graphite fiber is usually used in conjunction with epoxy resin. Epoxy resin is more flexible than polyester resin and has the unique property of increasing in strength as it ages.

Chemically activated polyester fabric was developed by the Noah Company for the fiber reinforced plastics industry. The manufacturer characterizes CAP as an impact modifier which is used in a similar manner to fiberglass or Kevlar.

Another type of fiberglass that has been used by sailboat, waterski, and aircraft manufacturers for some time is "S" glass. Not only does "S" glass contain more fibers per strand than ordinary fiberglass, but, unlike regular fberglass, each fiber in "S" glass is unbroken throughout its entire length. This makes each strand that the cloth is woven from stronger and stiffer. The weave of the cloth is also tighter than regular fiberglass. This cloth makes for a stronger shell than regular fiberglass, but it is harder to saturate, wrap around tight corners, and lay into the corners of channels.

E cloth is the fiberglass most commonly used in the surfboard industry. K glass (made in the U.S.A.) is unique among the cloths previously mentioned in that it has a flat weave rather than a twist weave. Voltex, (V glass from Japan) is a 4.8 ounce cloth which utilizes a thicker flat weave strand on the warp and a thinner twist strand on the welp (fill). The advantage to a flat weave is that it is saturated by a thinner, lighter layer of resin.

In the quest for lighter boards, some shapers have turned to expanded polystyrene foam. Eps foam is normally used with epoxy resin, as the styrene present in polyester resin dissolves the foam. The eps foam has a larger cell structure than polyurethane foam which makes it harder for a shaper to maintain fine details in a blank. The blanks are so light, that a soft weight is placed upon them during shaping to hold them down. In addition, because they are stringerless, the blanks flex while being shaped. Shapers accustomed to a stringer for visual reference usually score or snap a line on the blank. Proponents of eps foam and epoxy resin systems maintain that the shaped blanks are so light that the weight of the fiberglass laminate skin can be increased. This creates a stronger, lighter board with the concentration of weight in the outer skin. The drawback to using eps foam is that it absorbs water, so dings must be sealed immediately. In addition the epoxy resins have particular working properties that glassers used to polyester resin must familiarize themselves with, in order to use them successfully.

Eps blanks are cut from big blocks of the foam. Their rocker and thickness flow is cut by computer/camera controlled hot wire machines. This makes it easy to adapt blanks to changes in design. A Japanese company has developed a blank from extruded polystyrene foam. Called X-Tune (Crosstune), it has higher compressive strength, greater resistance to water absorbtion and a smaller cell structure than the expanded polystyrene foam. The smaller cell structure of this foam results in shaping properties that are similar to those of polyurethane foam.

These materials have properties that make them attractive to innovative and experimental construction techniques. Various resins, such as vinylester, and epoxy further influence their properties. Sometimes various types of fiber cloth are combined in layers to create a skin superior to any single type of cloth. These composite structures can make a board extremely light and very strong. As more sophisticated construction techniques and materials develop, specialized shapes will evolve for ultra-light boards. Prohibitive prices, toxicity, or ease of workability keep these products out of the mainstream of surfboard construction.

Ding Repair

1. Clean the area to be repaired of wax and sand, then rinse it with fresh water and let it dry thoroughly. Moisture can hinder the hardening of the resin and causes a white discoloration of the resin to occur. Wipe down all areas you plan to work on with acetone to remove traces of oil, wax and dirt.

2. Break away badly-shattered and delaminated glass. (see illustration A)

3. If the damage is less than one-quarter of an inch deep, it can be built-up with glass and resin. Automotive body filler with microballoons can also be used on shallow dings. If the damage is deeper than one-quarter of an inch, it is better to fill the ding with foam so that you don't add excess weight to the board. Resin and catalyst function best in temperatures of 70° F. Follow the manufacturers recommendations for the correct resin/catalyst relationship to insure adequate working time. Warmer temperatures speed up the chemical reaction whereas cooler temperatures slow it down. Don't try to hurry the hardening time of the resin by heating the repair in sunlight. Ultra Violet rays present in sunlight are a form of energy which encourage change in chemical structures influencing durability, appearance, or working properties.

4. When a major piece is taken out of your board, smooth the damaged area as much as possible with a rasp or coarse file. File into undamaged glass and foam one-sixteenth to one-eighth of an inch. (see illustration B)

5. Shape a piece of foam that perfectly fits the contour that you have created by smoothing out the damaged area. Brush the dust away from the damaged area. Apply masking tape ¼″ away from the edge of the ding all the way around it. Mix up some surfacing resin and catalyst and use it to glue in the plug that you have shaped for the damaged area. (see illustration C)

6. Once the resin has set up and the plug is securely in place use a surform to blend the foam into the surrounding contours of the board. A surform will skate over the undamaged surface of the area surrounding the ding without scratching it. With very light pressure on the surform you will get a nice finish on the foam. Let the tool do the work. Proceed with the surform until you get the foam to match the original contours as closely as possible. (see illustration D)

Ding Repair

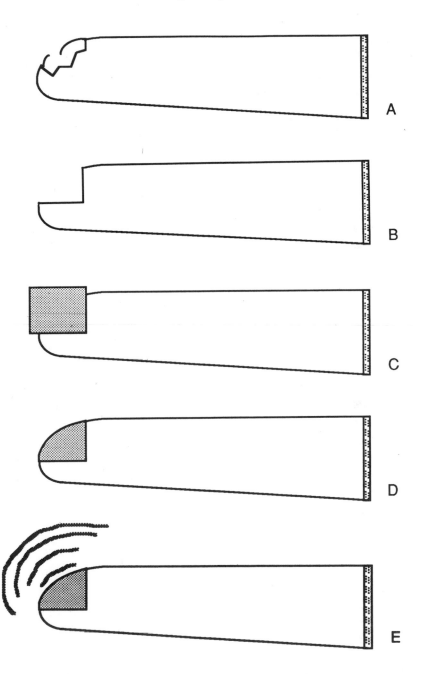

Ding Repair

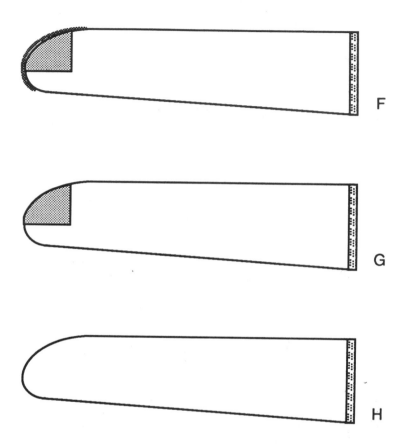

F

G

H

7. Use 100 grit sandpaper to shape the foam into as smooth a plug as possible. Once you get it flush take the foam down another one-sixteenth inch to allow room to build up fiberglass cloth. Make sure the gloss of the undamaged area around the foam plug is sanded with 50 or 60 grit sandpaper. This will insure that the resin and glass you apply during the repair will bond as well as possible. *(see illustration E)*

8. Tape off the ding ¼″ into the sanded area. Bend a ledge into the tape so that excess resin won't run all over the rest of the board. Position the board so that gravity will help keep the cloth in place.

9. Match the color of the board as closely as possible with artists' acrylics. There are hundreds of colors to choose from. The acrylic coated foam will darken in appearance when covered with glass and resin.

10. Cut out four layers of fiberglass cloth. The first layer put down should be about 1" smaller than the area to the tape on all sides. Each successive layer should be ¼" larger all the way around. The last layer should come all the way to the inside edge of the tape all the around. Set all these pieces out in order. Saturate the foam with catalized laminating resin and start applying the cloth. Use gloved fingers to saturate the cloth. The cloth is properly saturated when it becomes transparent. *(see illustration E)*

11. After the cloth has become tacky, brush surfacing resin over it. Let this set up until jelled, then pull the tape and let it set up hard and tack free. *(see illustration F)*

12. Sand the area flush with the area surrounding it using 120 grit paper. If you want to match existing color work, do it now by taping off the design and applying a thin layer of acrylic. Let the acrylic dry thoroughly. *(see illustration G)*

13. Tape off the sanded area and brush on gloss resin. When the resin jells pull the tape and let it set up hard. Sand this area with 320, 400 then 600 wet sand paper. You shouldn't be able to feel any lumps or ridges. Blend it in perfectly with a sanding block. For a final gloss apply automotive rubbing and polishing compounds by hand or with a buffing bonnet on a drill. *(see illustration H)*

If you are more concerned with a quick, smooth watertight repair than cosmetics, use surfacing resin rather than laminating resin to saturate the cloth, and immediately cover the repair with waxed paper. Put the waxed paper down against the wet, saturated glass before the resin starts to harden. The waxed paper should be as flat and smooth as possible. Work any air bubbles out to the edge as when applying a sticker or decal. The waxed paper allows the resin to fill in the texture of the cloth, creating a smooth repair in one step.

Evaluating the Condition of a Surfboard

The following are types of damage/"dings" you should look for when evaluating the condition of a board. If the damaged area is hard and watertight—my advice is to leave it alone.

1. Shatter-An area that has been bumped/flexed yet bounced back to its original contour; integrity, strength, and watertight quality of the shattered area is virtually uneffected.

2. Dent-Permanent compression of the foam/fiberglass; numerous dents are typically found on the deck (due to knee and heel pressure) and are often accompanied by crescent shaped cracks (in the sand/gloss coats) along the stringer. Cracks should be sanded out and sealed by restoring watertight sand/gloss coats.

3. Bump/Soft Spot-Indicates delamination (breakdown of the foam/fiberglass bond); can be fixed by drilling two small holes at opposite ends of the delaminated area (one to let resin in and the other to let air out) injecting catalized resin under the glass using a wallpaper hanger's syringe (making sure to move the board around so that the resin penetrates completely) covering the area with waxed paper and weighing it down until resin cures to restore the foam/fiberglass bond.

4. Ding-A break in the fiberglass that exposes foam (allowing it to absorb water) and compromises strength; should be fixed to restore strength and keep the board watertight.

5. Stress Cracks-Cracks in the gloss/sand coats often accompanied by shatters that run across the bottom of the board (approximately 90° to the stringer); indicate that the board was severely flexed and possibly came very close to breaking in half; Check the deck opposite the cracks for delamination—if it is present, one more direct hit will probably break the board.

6. Fins/Glass-on Fins/Finboxes-Fins typically sustain damage (nicks) on leading or trailing edges which can be (built up with resin and glass if necessary) sanded and refoiled. Cracks up the side of the fin indicate that it has been severely flexed, but since fins are typically solid glass/resin this doesn't need to be fixed. A few cracks or shatters at the base of a glass-on fin aren't too bad if the fin is solid, however if there are a lot of cracks or shatters, and you can detect any delamination, or the fin is loose, the fin will require removal, restoration of it's attachment point and reattachment. Cracks in or around fin boxes will absorb water.

7. Nose/Tail Damage-The tip of the nose and tail are often bumped, crushed, or scraped; these areas should be kept watertight (you can seal a damaged nose tip with a Nose Guard) because the foam and wooden stringer will absorb water.

Wetsuits

Fit – A wetsuit is designed to let water in, hence the name. The amount of water that the suit lets in is determined by how closely it fits. A thin layer of water is trapped between you and the suit. Your body heat warms up that water to keep you warm. Ideally, the wetsuit should fit like a second skin, snug everywhere without being constrictive. Different brands cut and size their suits in different ways, and offer a wide variety of styles. Get the suit that fits you best. Most of the major brands use top quality materials and construction techniques so one brand won't wear much better than another. If you get a suit that doesn't fit well, it will allow pockets of water to accumulate against your body. Everytime you punch through a wave or fall off your board you will face a cold agonizing flush. Don't compromise on fit. If you don't fit into a stock size it is worth the slight extra charge to order a custom. When trying a wetsuit on be aware of the zipper and seams and how they feel against your skin. Flex the suit through your full range of normal surfing movements. Suits that bind or chafe should be avoided.

Seams – Seams should be as smooth, supple and watertight as possible. All seams should be intelligently placed so that they don't cause uncomfortable binding or chafing when the suit is on for long periods. The number of seams should be kept to a minimum. Usually, zig-zag stitching is used for collars, cuffs and edges. Blind stitching is preferable because the material is only stitched halfway through – eliminating stitch holes through the suit that let water in. The material used on some warm water wetsuits doesn't lend itself to blind stitching techniques. Overlock stitches join the seam in a coil manner that enhances stretchability without compromising strength. Most seams are glued as well as stitched – some manufacturers use a tape bonded to the inside of the seam and glue on the seam itself to eliminate stitching altogether.

Thickness – Surfing wetsuits are usually ⅛ inch (about 3 mm) in thickness. Specialty materials vary from .5 mm to 5 mm. Several thicknesses of material are often used in the same suit so that the torso is insulated by thick rubber while joints maintain freedom with thin rubber. The basic things to remember are that suits made with thicker rubber are warmer because they have more of an insulating effect, but their thickness restricts freedom of movement. Thinner wetsuits aren't as warm, but restrict movement less. Rubber with a small grid pattern texture on the exterior is slightly more flexible than the usual smooth rubber exterior. Pick a suit style with a seam cut and zipper placement that won't bind or chafe through your full range of surfing movements. Some full suits zip straight up the backbone, while others utilize a turtle neck with the zipper across the shoulders or on the chest. If the neck feels too tight, fold it inside, this gives you more slack. Also, the smooth rubber is less irritating to beards. Pick the suit that compliments your metabolism and gives you the best compromise between warmth and flexibility.

Styles – There are many different styles of wetsuits. One piece suits with long and short sleeve or leg lengths, high or low necks, and various thicknesses of rubber are available. Suits with zippers placed across the shoulders, or across the upper chest are looser in the shoulder area so that the zipper (which doesn't stretch) won't restrict paddling motion. For this reason, suits with zippers placed straight up the back can fit the shoulders closer. Various rubber thicknesses are available to provide you with the ideal combination of warmth and flexibility for any condition.

The question of warmth vs. flexibility will often come up. Some people say they would rather surf for less time, and be free to move. Others maintain that if you aren't warm, you can't move anyway. You are the best judge of what is right for you.

Booties, vests, hoods and gloves should fit especially snug. If booties are the least bit loose they fill up with water and it feels as though you have water balloons on your feet. If a vest fits loosely, when you wipe out it may slide up around your arms and shoulders hindering your ascent to the surface. Hoods help a great deal in retaining body heat. They should fit well and feel comfortable to move in. Hoods are excellent in case you have to punch through waves on cold days; they spare you that agonizing "ice cream" headache sensation. Hoods also keep your ears covered protecting them from cold wind and water. Used in conjunction with Doc's Pro Plugs (see personal equipment), hoods may be quite useful in protecting the cold water surfer from developing surfer's ear.

Using different styles, cuts, and zipper placements as well as various thicknesses of rubber in the construction of wetsuits can improve heat retention and flexibility. Thicker rubber can be used in the torso area for warmth and thinner rubber may be used at the shoulders, knees and arms for increased flexibility and paddling ease. Other non-rubber materials such as nylon, gortex, or lycra can be used in specific areas of the wetsuit to create a more flexible suit.

Nylon II - Nylon bonded to the neoprene is the material lining the inside of your suit. You will also find the nylon on exterior areas that are particularly susceptible to abrasive wear. Some suits are constructed from Nylon II, and are nylon lined inside and out. The Nylon II suit is more expensive and lasts longer than its regular counterpart. The Nylon retains more water, which makes it slightly heavier and more cumbersome than regular neoprene. It also looses more heat due to evaporation. As the wind blows against the saturated nylon, the evaporation cools the suit and you; 3mm smoothskin is about as warm as 5 mm Nylon II because of this evaporation factor. Nylon II has almost the same flexibility as one-sided Nylon because the smooth skin has a more dense layer of rubber on the outside. Some companies have used lycra as a substitute for Nylon II. Lycra is lighter, and absorbs less water than Nylon II but isn't as flexible.

Upkeep - When you peel your wetsuit off, roll it inside out. Never take a wetsuit off by pulling at the end of a sleeve and trying to slide an arm out. Always let it roll off inside out. Everytime you use the wetsuit, rinse it in fresh water. Leave the suit inside out and hang it on a wooden or plastic hanger so that it will dry. Stay away from metal hangers because they rust. By letting the suit dry inside out, the part that will be touching your skin will always be as comfortable as possible. Try not to leave the suit creased for more than a day at a time. Folds are hard on the rubber. If you must pack your wetsuit, roll it up rather than folding it.

If you happen to tear the suit or split a seam, take care of it as soon as possible. The wetsuit is a stressed skin which will continually pull at any tear left unfixed. Tie off any unravelled seam threads to themselves so they can't unravel further. After the suit has been rinsed and is dry, apply two layers of wetsuit glue (a special type of contact cement) to each side of the tear. After the surface of the glue has dried to the point of being only slightly tacky, press both sides firmly together. You can sew your suit with a strong synthetic thread. Stiff or excessively thin threads will tear through the rubber. Keep in mind that the seam or repair has to flex so try to use the same type of stitch that was in the seam originally.

There are patches available to repair wetsuits that are ironed into place onto Nylon II. These patches are made from the same material that some manufacturers use to seal seams. The advantage to using on iron-on patch to repair your suit rather than sewing it up, is that you avoid creating holes in the suit that will let water in.

Your dealer can send your suit back to the factory for complete reconditioning. The factories do excellent zipper replacement, repairs, and reconditioning at very reasonable prices.

Rash Guards – Regardless of how well your suit fits, if you're out in the water for long sessions several days in a row, you're going to develop a rash. In the past, the only remedy was a thick layer of Vaseline over the raw spot and a "grin and bear it" attitude. Several wetsuit companies are now making ultra thin, light, flexible, rash guards. They're made from Lycra, and cut in several styles (vest, t-shirt, t-shirt w/high neck). Rash guards fit like a second skin, and allow you to move within your suit with less resistance. They virtually eliminate chafing and keep you warmer by minimizing the amount of water that moves through your suit.

Note: The best tip I can offer for surfing cold conditions is to take a five gallon container of hot tap water with you when you go to the beach. The water cools down to a comfortable temperature while you're surfing and you get a rejuvenating warm shower when you come in.

Personal Equipment

Wax – Wax is rubbed onto the deck for traction. Wax is formulated for different water temperatures. Harder wax is for warmer waters. Even in cooler climates it is best to use a hard wax for a base coat so that your wax won't melt off if exposed to warm termperatures.

Wax is rubbed on in long, even strokes. By using the thin edge of the bar with light to moderate pressure, a good traction surface consisting of small round beads will build up. Once the beads start to build up, alternate strokes ninety degrees so they stay small and round. Using the flat side of the bar or applying the wax with excessive pressure will cause it to smear on. This will result in long wax scabs that flake off easily. Wax will also smear if it heats up too much from the friction created during application; you'll get a better job if you take your time. A soft wax can be applied over a hard wax, but if you try to apply a hard wax over a soft, the soft wax gets scraped off.

If you find yourself at the beach without any wax, rough up the surface with a comb. If your wax has built up too thick, just use the comb for awhile. Keep sand off your wax for it creates an abrasive surface for skin and wetsuits.

Wax can easily be removed after it is softened or melted by leaving the board in the sun or by rinsing the board with hot water. Apply as little heat to your board as possible to minimize the risk of delamination. Carefully scrape the softened wax off the deck with a pliable plastic squeegee that won't scratch the deck of your board.

Wax Free Traction Surfaces – Wax free traction surfaces are available in both spray and stick on varieties. The spray is a wax substitute that is sprayed on a clean deck. The stick on traction pads come in various sizes, shapes, colors, finishes and thicknesses. They come with an adhesive backing and are applied directly to a clean deck. You continue to use wax around the pads. The pads are usually placed to give the rear foot maximum traction and control, however some surfers use them for the front foot as well. The padded type cushions knee and heel pressure to minimize deck denting. Pick the texture that suits your needs, keeping in mind whether you will be using the board exclusively with a wetsuit, or whether your skin will also be contacting the surface. Pick a pad shape that is least likely to trip you up. Thicker pads are also available in various shapes that your rear foot can locate against to further enhance your control.

Sunscreen – Sunlight contains ultra-violet rays that can cause sunburn, premature aging and worst of all skin cancer. Waterproof sunscreens have been developed and formulated to stay on your skin and provide ultra sun protection while you surf. There are two types of sunscreen. The absorbers, which are absorbed into the skin and the reflectors which stay on top of the skin.

The absorbers are available in paba, paba derived or non paba formulations. If your skin is sensitive to paba, use formulations that contain benzophenone or cinnanate. Absorbers are so named because they are absorbed into the skin. Since they're absorbed into the skin they stay on better and function longer than reflectors. Absorbers are most effective if applied 20-30 minutes before going in the water. You'll get better protection by putting them on well in advance (not as you're waxing up – ready to charge into the water) onto skin that isn't sweaty. When you sweat, fluid is coming out of your skin which makes it harder for the absorbers to get in.

The reflectors are actual sunblocks – barriers that work on top of the skin. These are typically formulated from zinc oxide or titanium dioxide. The problem with the reflectors is that they can be wiped off, leaving skin unprotected.

The SPF number is a sun protection factor rating and indicates the degree of protection the sunscreen provides. Higher numbers indicate longer protection from the sun's rays.

Current research clearly shows that skin cancer tends to appear in areas that have peeled or blistered due to sunburn. Your goal in using a sunblock or sunscreen should be to avoid sunburn. There are several types of skin cancer that can be treated with only cosmetic disfigurement as a consequence. However there is a life threatening form of skin cancer which all surfers should be aware of. It is called malignant melanoma, appears as a new mole, and can be identified with this simple A.B.C.D. test.

A. Asymmetry; one half of the mole doesn't match the other half
B. Border; the border is irregular
C. Color; the mole will have more than one color on it
D. Diameter; any mole larger than one quarter of an inch in diameter should be watched very closely – if it grows at all, it should be checked by a dermatologist.

Sunglasses – Even though sunglasses are often regarded as a fashion statement, it is important to remember that their primary function is to protect your eyes. Bloodshot eyes, eye strain, eye pain, headaches, fatigue and temporary blindness are some of the symptoms of short term overexposure to the sun. It is also suspected that long term overexposure to the sun can cause retinal deterioration and may promote the fleshy growths of pterygia and pinguecula. Pterygia extends into the cornea where it can obstruct vision and erode the corneal surface. Pinguecula is similar but less extensive and usually stays on the sclera (white) of the eye. Just as you wear a sunscreen to protect your skin from ultraviolet rays, you want to make sure that the sunglasses you choose offer 100% protection from ultraviolet rays. The sparkles on the ocean surface are concentrated rays of sun directed towards the eyes. As surfers, the time we spend looking out over the water with our eyes unprotected is all the more reason to take good care of them whenever possible. Whatever sunglasses you choose, be sure they have shatter-proof lenses that are optically perfect for distortion free vision. If you have a pair of sunglasses that you're unsure about, have them tested at an optician's office. They have meters that can measure the amount of ultraviolet, infrared and visible light your lenses let through so you can be sure your eyes are getting the protection they require.

People with extremely sun sensitive eyes that limit their ability to remain near the water during peak sun periods – may benefit from Suntacts. Developed by William Petersen, O.D. of Dana Point, California, Suntacts (available in prescription or non prescription) utilize a high concentration of the green pigment used in cosmetically tinted lenses to eliminate glare and cut harmful ultraviolet rays by 84%-87%.

Pro Plugs – Many surfers who have been surfing for over four years have developed a condition called "surfer's ear." Surfer's ear occurs when the bone in the ear canal is irritated by cold water and air. Cold or warm air blowing over wet skin lowers the temperature by evaporation, thus stimulating bony growth even in the tropics. Lower temperatures cause blood vessels to constrict, decreasing the blood and oxygen supply to the bone. This irritates the bone and causes the bone to grow.

"Doc's Pro Plugs" protect the ear canal by keeping a warm pocket of air in the canal. They keep cold water out without impeding hearing or balance. Doctor Scott's valve, a hole in the inner diaphram, allows the transfer of air and thus sound waves and differences in air pressure. Most water will not pass through the hole due to surface tension. Anyone with severe narrowing of the ear canal can avoid frequent blockage by wearing Pro Plugs. Latest research suggest that severe exostosis (surfer's ear) is reversible by keeping the ears religiously warm around the clock with plugs and woolen head bands or hats. For comfort, use one size smaller Pro Plug on land than you would normally wear in the water.

Dr. Scott has observed in surfers with severe exostosis that the process of bone growth goes on during the rest of the day and especially during cold nights while sleeping. By keeping the ears warm with Pro Plugs, you can avoid the inconvenience of surfer's ear. This reversal of the bony growth by heat conservation is very important medically, as previously the only recourse was to submit to a microsurgical drilling-out procedure costing about $2,500.00 per ear. Convalescense required about six weeks out of the water. Once drilled out, the bony growth seems to grow back even more rapidly when exposed to the cold. In addition to being very comfortable, the plugs offer invaluable protection in the prevention of ruptured ear drums.

Leashes – Leashes should be a minimum of six feet long. If the leash is too short the board remains dangerously close to you throughout the turmoil of a wipeout. The larger the waves you want to use a leash in, the longer the leash should be. I have heard of leashes up to twenty five feet in length being used in large island waves. The longer leashes minimize pull and impact, and are less prone to breakage. Use leashes that are strong enough to deal with the kinds of waves you ride. A leash that is too long allows your board to get too far away after a wipeout. This makes it difficult to reach your board before successive waves are upon you. An excessively long leash increases the risk to other surfers which may be near you.

Occasionally leashes tangle on the bottom or in something and keep you from reaching the surface. For this reason, pick a leash that utilizes an uncomplicated ankle strap that can be unfastened quickly and easily. If your leash does get caught on something and you can't get to the surface make sure you reach down to remove your ankle strap with both hands, so you're sure to get it off on the first try. You may not get a second chance.

Always try to surf as though you are not using a leash. Regard the leash as a convenience rather than a necessity. Broken urethane leashes can be repaired. Heat the broken ends until they melt and become pliable. Do not let the ends overheat or catch fire for the resulting carbon residue will destroy the bonding capabilities of the urethane. When the urethane is pliable and melted at the ends, firmly push the broken ends together and quench the repaired joint in cold water to anneal the urethane and insure a strong bond.

Rail Savers – Whenever you use a leash you should also use a rail saver. The rail saver is a flat nylon strap 1 or 2 inches wide and 8-10 inches in length. The rail saver is attached between the board and the leash. Rail savers distribute the force of a violently pulled leash over a wider area on the rail so that the leash will not tear through the rail.

Nose Guard – The nose guard is a soft, silicone, shock absorbing bumper that is glued onto the nose tip of contemporary boards. Island Classic Surfboards shaper Eric Arakawa and partner David Skedeleski took a year to develop the product with input from Hawaii's top surfers and shapers. They developed the nose guard because of the increasing number of injuries from pointed nose tips. The softness of the nose guard improves the safety of blunted noses as well.

Surfer/Surfboard Attachments – Several different products have been introduced over the years to attach the surfer to the surfboard. Velcro was strapped to the feet and would match up with a strategically placed compliment glued to the board. Booties with suction cups on the sole would stick the surfer to an unwaxed deck. Another product along these lines is a front foot strap. A strap is anchored on the board 90 degrees to the stringer. As the surfer rides the wave, the foot is slipped in under this strap. Turning the foot to its normal position diagonal to the stringer, twists and tightens the strap.

   A mechanical union between surfer and board has the potential of greatly influencing both maneuvers and surfboard design. Aerials, stalls, and with the help of speed, various maneuvers that defy gravity, can be imagined. The size, power, predictability and intensity of the surf determines the safety of such devices. The detrimental effects these devices pose to comfortably making subtle adjustments in position and balance during critical situations has limited their use.

Gloves – Webbed gloves are available that increase the area of your hand and offer improved grip on your board. The increased area that the gloves provide improve the effectiveness of your paddling stroke, allowing you to paddle faster. This improves your ability to get into waves early and position yourself more effectively. The increased resistance they create builds paddling strength. The gloves offer excellent protection for your hands when surfing extremely shallow reefs, especially if you're caught inside and have to grab the reef. When using webbed gloves, you may find that you have to alter your hand placement or finger positioning, to keep the water that's rushing by from peeling your hand off the rail.

Pro-Lite Travel Cases – The founders of Pro-Lite, Dave Neilsen and Bill Hapgood, are both former airline employees. They are familiar with the way surfboards are handled by baggage carriers and have done extensive research into the best way to protect a surfboard. Their one, two and three board cases are lightweight, durable, and easy to use. They have developed a foam fin block that fits over and protects vulnerable glassed on tri fins. The shoulder strap makes carrying your board comfortable. The zipper entry allows you to pack or unpack your board in a minute. If you are serious about traveling with a surfboard, make it easy on yourself and safe for your board. Pro-Lite has defined the leading edge of protective luggage for surfing equipment.

Harvest Surfboard Protectors – Harvest, a Japanese company, has developed a set of molded rubber bumpers that fit on vulnerable rail, nose and tail areas of surfboards. They offer extra protection for the areas of the surfboard that are most likely to be damaged in transit. I've found them to be an excellent compliment to the Pro-Lite case.

Important Qualities of Your First Surfboard

Acquiring the strength and wave judgment to surf takes time. Experienced surfers make the sport look easy because they've spent years learning about and adapting to the ocean. When surfing, the ocean is in control and a lack of wave knowledge is a great disadvantage. This makes it all the more important to pick a board that will make up for your weaknesses rather than compounding them. Your first surfboard should float well, paddle easily, catch waves early, and be as stable as possible.

Length – Your first surfboard should be about fourteen inches longer than your height.

Width – A minimum width of twenty inches is essential for paddling, stability, and wave catching ease. Increased width will improve planing efficiency and stability in the smaller, slower surf ideal for beginners.

Template – A full or wider than normal template is best for a first board. A standard outline with wider than normal dimensions will be an advantage to you. Don't get a board with an extremely pointed nose because pointed noses are dangerous. If you already have a board with a pointed nose, put a Nose Guard on it. It doesn't make sense to risk injury from a design feature that doesn't benefit performance. Your board should be as versatile as possible so that it is suitable for the wide range of conditions you will be subjecting it to. Also, if the board is versatile, you don't have to make up for its faults. It will carry you through whatever you are up against with the greatest of ease.

Tail Design – Your first surfboard should have a blunt tail design such as a round, rounded square or squash tail. Since you are just beginning to deal with new sensations, you won't be able to discern one tail design from another. You will have your hands full with paddling, catching waves, and trying to stand up. Pin tails and swallow tails increase the risk of injury without benefitting the learning process. Even if you catch on to surfing very quickly, it will be at least one year before you can discern one tail design from another. Stay with something safe.

Thickness – Thickness of the board should be a minimum of ½ inch per twenty-five pounds of body weight in the thickest part of the board. Maximum board thickness is usually about three and one half inches. If you are heavy, turn to extra width for additional flotation.

Soft Boards – Soft boards offer an excellent alternative for the beginner. They are made in shapes ideally suited to beginners. Since they are soft, the risk of injury is greatly reduced. They won't ding at a time when you're getting used to dealing with the cumbersome size of a surfboard. Soft boards are your safest alternative at a time when you are most vulnerable to being hit by your board.

Modern Mini Longboards – Modern mini longboards such as the Eatons pictured in the Design Section, are a great investment for the beginner. They paddle easily, catch waves early, are very stable and maneuver really well for their size. A modern longboard can be purchased with the confidence that you'll never outgrow it's use. As you progress you can still take it out on small days or when you want a change of pace. They are also great to have around when you want to introduce a friend to surfing.

If you're serious about learning how to surf, choosing the best board to learn on is the most important thing you can do. The right board will get you through the awkward beginner's stage as quickly and easily as possible. The design specifications of boards suitable for beginners remain fairly constant, evolve slowly, and are universally understood by experienced shapers. This is because everyone that goes through the beginning process, can relate to the beginner's needs, and because beginners (except for size variation) typically require the same attributes from a board. For these reasons the modern mini longboards hold onto their value and are easy to sell. Resist the temptation to buy an oversized version of what you think you'll be riding in the future, with the thought of struggling a little more at first but coming out ahead in the long run. Surfing is difficult enough to learn with everything in your favor. Even with the right equipment, you'll find surfing a difficult sport to master. Trying to learn on equipment you'll "grow into", may keep you from ever learning at all. In addition, you'll probaby find that the oversized version of the "latest" design you compromised on a year ago is outdated, obsolete, hard to sell, and even you don't want it anymore. When you compromise on your surfboard, you inevitably compromise your surfing. Your surfboard plays a tremendous role in the development of your surfing ability; chose it carefully.

Buying a Used Surfboard – When shopping for any board (new or used), define your needs and find a board that will satisfy them. Don't compromise on your requirements from a board just because of price. An inexpensive board that doesn't suit your needs is a poor value. If you're beginning, choose increased volume (longer, wider, thicker) over decreased volume (shorter, narrower, thinner), make sure nose and tail are blunt, and remember that you only need one fin. There are a lot of nice looking boards and it's easy to be swayed to equipment that doesn't suit your needs if you don't have a clear dimensional sense of your requirements. Shapers are continually refining and improving board designs so you're usually better off with a newer board. Stick to reputable "name" brands and experienced shapers you can trust. Once you've found a suitable board, remove any wax (wax can hide damage on the deck), clean the board and examine it carefully. Stay away from boards that: aren't watertight; have a lot of dings or poorly executed repairs; are waterlogged (abnormally heavy with discolored brown foam and dings that ooze water when they're pushed); have sustained severe damage (large stress cracked/shattered/delaminated areas or have been broken and put back together). Specific types of damage you should look for when evaluating the condition of a surfboard are outlined in the Ding Repair section.

Waves

One day you may wonder what waves are and how they are created. There is an excellent book on this subject by a man named Willard Bascom.[1] I will now provide you with a basic explanation.

Most of the waves we see and ride are created by wind. As the wind blows against the water, ripples are formed. Ripples offer the wind a more efficient surface to push against. As the energy is transferred from wind to water more efficiently, the ripples grow. When ripples grow too steep they break, creating whitecaps. A wave which is seven feet long will break when it reaches a height of one foot. A seventy foot long wave will break at a height of ten feet. Longer waves are more stable.

As the whitecaps break, part of their energy is absorbed by the turbulence, but a majority of it goes into the creation of longer waves. The longer, more stable waves accept yet more wind energy. A particular velocity of wind is capable of producing a particular size of wave. Whether or not maximum wave heights are reached by a particular velocity of wind depends on two other factors: (1) the length of time which the wind blows; and (2) the amount of area that the wind has to act upon the water (the fetch).

When the waves are no longer influenced by the wind, they blend into smooth, long swells. Swells can travel thousands of miles across deep water at twenty to seventy miles per hour with very little energy loss. The swell moves from the area in which it was created in trains which are made up of groups of waves. The trains are made up of energy transferred from wind to ocean. The swell slows down as it travels because energy is needed to mobilize water particles in its path. As leading waves disappear from this mobilization process, new ones appear at the rear.

The swells that reach a distant shore are distant offshoots of the original sea. The water is merely the medium which makes the original wind energy apparent to us. Waves are pure energy. The water that the wind originally blew upon never reaches shore. The phenomena of waves is similar to the actions of a whip. Your arm provides the energy to the handle. The energy travels the length of the whip and strikes the ground. The whip responds to your energy as the sea responds to the wind.

[1]William Bascom, Waves and Beaches – The Dynamics of the Ocean Surface, New York (1964). Published by Anchor Books, Doubleday & Co.

As the waves reach water roughly 1.3 times their height they start to break. If the swells travelling in the open ocean hit abrupt reefs, as in the Hawaiian Islands, they break very quickly and with tremendous force. If the swells are slowed down by a continental shelf and gently sloping bottom, they break with less force.

Swells, like winds, are named for the direction from which they come. South swells travel from south to north. North swells travel from north to south and so on. Swells of a particular direction can be expected from seasonal storm systems in areas where the swell is created. California receives south swells during the summer from winter storms south of the equator. Hawaii's awesome winter waves are the result of storms in the North Pacific.

An indication of the distance swells have traveled is the time interval between waves. Pick a spot in the water and time how long it takes for ten waves (breaking or not) to pass by that spot. Divide that time by ten and you have the time interval between waves. Shorter time intervals between waves indicate a local swell with close proximity. Longer time intervals between sets indicate a swell that has traveled great distance. Swells where waves have a frequency greater than fifteen seconds have originated from storm systems that are at least 3,000 miles away.

At the beginning of a swell, the waves with a longer time interval between them will arrive first. Waves with a shorter period between them will arrive at the end of a swell because waves of a shorter frequency travel slower than waves of a longer frequency.

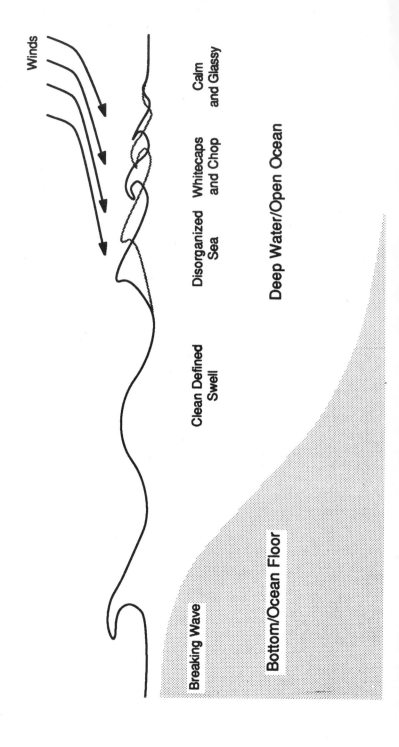

How Waves are Created by the Wind

Winds

Calm and Glassy

Whitecaps and Chop

Disorganized Sea

Deep Water/Open Ocean

Clean Defined Swell

Breaking Wave

Bottom/Ocean Floor

84

Winds

Winds are named for the direction from which they blow. A north wind will blow from the north to the south. A west wind will blow from the west to the east. A south wind will blow from the south to north. An east wind will blow from the east to the west. Variations in the wind direction are described by using compass points as well, such as northwest (blowing from the northwest) or southeast (blowing from the southeast), etc. A description such as south-southwest would indicate that the wind is predominately south, with a bit of southwest in it. Learn which winds are prevalent in the area where you surf, how particular storm systems and seasonal changes influence the winds, and how changes in wind direction effect wave quality on the stretch of coast you surf.

Offshore winds blow from land out to sea. These winds are the most favorable for surfing because they hold up the face of the wave.

Sideshore winds blow parallel to the waves. If they blow into the tube they'll hold the wave up and the tube open with an effect similar to that of an offshore wind. If they blow from the peak, down the line, they will cause the wave to break ahead of itself, creating slight chop and bump on the face similar to an onshore wind.

Onshore winds blow from the sea to land. Onshore winds usually render the waves unsurfable. Kelp will smooth chop created by slight onshore winds.

The lack of any wind allows the surface of the water to become very calm and glassy.

Winds are usually calm or offshore in the early morning and evening. The reason for this is because of the temperature difference between land and sea. The sea remains a constant temperature varying little between day and night. Land cools substantially at night, and is warmed by the sun during the day. The air over the water keeps a constant temperature while the air over the land cools at night and heats up during the day. Cool air is more dense and heavier than warm air. When the air over the land is cooler than the air over the sea, the airflow, or wind, is offshore. When the air over the sea is cooler than the air over the land, the airflow, or wind, is onshore. Local storm and geographic conditions may alter these effects.

Tides

The gravitational attraction of the moon and sun upon the earth cause tides. The gravitational forces create a wave that has a period (distance between crests) of 12 hrs. 25 min. and a wave length of half the circumference of the earth. The crest of this wave is high tide and the trough is low tide. The wave remains stationary while beneath it the earth spins on its' axis as it makes a complete rotation once a day. This is why most points on earth experience two high and low tides a day. The moon's orbit is eliptical. The varience in the distance between the earth and moon during it's orbit (perigee = 15,000 mi. closer, apogee = 15,000 mi. further away) causes tides that are respectively 20% higher and lower than average. Tides are more radical during the full and new moon phases and at least twice a year a full or new moon exists at perigee to produce the highest tides of the year.

Each tide has a value placed on it. This value corresponds to an increase or decrease in feet over the mean or average low tide. Values are always plus (+) for high tides. Values for low tides can be (+) on average days or minus (-) for days of extreme low tides.

Tides change about every six hours. If there is a high tide at 6:00 a.m., you can expect the tide to go out, or ebb, to a low near noon. Then the tide will come in, or flood, until 6:00 p.m. Tidal currents can effect swell size. It's not uncommon for a swell to get a push and increase in size during an incoming tide or drop in size during an outgoing tide.

Most breaks work best on particular tides. The tide at which the spot works best can be discovered by asking a local surfer, surf shop, or by careful observation. Usually if the break is mushy or slow, a lower tide will make it break harder and faster. If the break is closing out or too fast to make, a higher tide may make it break slower. Tide tables for the week are usually published in the weather section of the local newspaper. Tide schedules for the year are available from most surf and fishing shops.

PROJECT Wipeout

Hoag Hospital

© 1986 HOAG HOSPITAL

Catchit

Preventing surf-related spinal cord injuries is the responsibility of each swimmer. Here are some important guidelines to help beach-goers stay safe in the surf.

- Don't run from the beach into the water and dive headfirst into the waves.
- If you're bodysurfing, always keep your arms out in front of you to protect your head and neck.
- Don't jump or dive into the water from a pier or rock jetty.
- Check with the lifeguard to find out where shallow and deep areas are located. Remember, the ocean floor is constantly shifting.
- If you're novice, don't tackle waves three feet high or higher.
- Don't swim in any area unless there's a lifeguard on duty.
- Don't swim or surf alone.
- Don't drink or use drugs at the beach.

Surfing Safely

Surfing safely requires awareness; a constant and accurate assessment of potential risk. Your ability to size up a situation and respond appropriately is essential. Checking out conditions, choosing your equipment, and positioning yourself in relation to the wave and other surfers is all your responsibility. To the beginner, surfing may seem totally free, almost anarchistic in nature. However, there is law; the law of the ocean, nature's law, which makes man's law seem trivial by comparison. Judgements are immediate and there's no appeal. On bigger days, even if you're out with a crowd, you feel one on one with the most untamed and powerful force on earth. You won't be able to intellectualize a solution to every situation you'll face in the sea. The sea works on a far more basic level than learned knowledge. Use all your senses and supplement knowledge with intuition. If you get a strong feeling about a situation, act on it and figure it out later. Experience will hone your sense and you'll learn when to push and when to back off. When you're out in the ocean every move has a consequence, the result, good or bad, is up to you.

There are a few things in the ocean that you should be aware of and avoid. Barracuda and a few of the 250 species of shark have been known to attack man. Sea snakes that possess a venom more potent than any snake on land inhabit the South Pacific and Indian Oceans. Lionfish and Scorpionfish (also known as rock and stone fish) are the most lethal poisonous fish. The scorpionfish lie among hollows in rocks and reef and have hypodermic-like spines on their dorsal fin. If stepped on, the spines are pushed onto venom filled sacks at their base injecting the victim with venom.

Sea urchins dwell in small hollows of reef and shelf where they are protected from waves. Eels inhabit small tunnels and caves. Jellyfish and sea anemones can cause very painful stings, and some jellyfish can even kill humans. The jellyfishes' tentacles continue injecting the victim with venom as long as they are in contact with the skin. Even a seemingly lifeless segment of jellyfish can sting. Do some research about your local waters and any areas you plan on traveling to so that you are aware of any potentially dangerous sea life common to the area.

As numerous as these natural hazards seem, your greatest risk comes from your equipment or another surfer. Rounding your nose and tail tip(s) as well as dulling the rear edge of your fin(s) can minimize your risk of injury. Make sure to use a leash of adequate length. Never paddle directly behind another surfer as a set approaches; get to one side of him or another even if it means taking a harder hit from the wave. If a surfer outside of you looses control of his board or breaks a leash, you run the risk of getting hit by his board. If you find yourself behind someone, let him know that you're there. It may inspire him to hold onto his board better. Inevitably leashes will break and boards will get loose. When it happens, watch the board for as long as you can; boards are often hidden in whitewater and make sudden changes of direction as they're pushed toward shore.

If you need any surf related health information, contact the Surfer's Medical Association, 2396 Great Highway/48th Avenue, San Francisco, California 94116, (415) 664-7027.

Some of the items I've found indispensible in my surf trip first aid kit are: (1) Betadine (2) alcohol (3) ace bandage (4) bandages and adhesive butterfly closures (5) a sterile blade (6) sunscreen (7) Vaseline to prevent wetsuit chafing (8) vanilla extract to discourage no-see-ems and (9) an aloe vera based lotion to soothe sunburned or irritated skin.

Some surf spots are more dangerous than others. Shallow water with rock or coral reef bottoms can be extremely dangerous. The shallow water causes the wave to break quicker, hollower, and with more power. This power can be a challenge to the experienced surfer who has spent years learning the ways of the ocean, but can be deadly to the novice.

Most breaks in tropical waters are caused by coral reefs. Old dead reef is often worn smooth by wave action. Living reef is often jagged and sharp. There may be areas where the coral creates tunnels, caves, crevaces and overhangs. If you're swept under an overhang during a wipeout, protect your head, open your eyes and pick your way out. The use of booties and gloves allows you to position yourself into crevaces or hollows in the reef and use them as a safe shelter if you're caught inside where it's extremely shallow.

The life cycle of coral, fish feeding off of it, and exposure to oceanic elements cause some areas of the reef to be extremely sharp. Most coral reefs are sharp enough to cut at the slightest touch. Coral is also covered with bacteria infested film that greatly increases the likelihood of infection. Do your best to avoid touching the reef. Sharp reef can lie a few feet off a sandy beach, hidden from you by foam or sand agitated by the shorebreak. Flip your board upside-down and paddle across shallow stretches of reef. As you paddle into the line up, watch the wave and note any places where it sucks out abruptly from encountering shallow water. Watch local surfers to see if they avoid any part of the wave or treat it conservatively. If they do, it's probably shallow there. If you fall, fall flat, like a belly flop on your back so you don't penetrate the water deeply and impale yourself on the reef. Wear wetsuit booties to protect your feet when surfing an especially shallow reef. Elastic ankle supports can be used to keep booties from filling with water and coming off your foot. If you do bump the reef, check yourself; you may be cut without realizing it. In Hawaii, applying Betadine to my cuts as soon as I got out of the water allowed them to heal normally. Don't be lax with coral cuts or any injury that breaks the skin if you are surfing alot. They can get overcome with staph and turn into raised ulcerated craters that are painful and take months to heal.

Rock shelf breaks are usually pretty flat. Rocks on top of sand and sand bottoms are also quite safe. Sand bottoms change a great deal. Various swell directions, tidal currents, or seasonal beach changes make the sand bottom very susceptible to change.

A reef, shelf, or sandbar that causes the wave to come into very shallow water from very deep water outside, causes the wave to break very quickly. Extremely shallow water creates boils and other deformities in the face of the wave.

Currents are fierce in some areas and almost non-existent in others. Watch the water. Currents or rips usually make themselves apparent with isolated areas of extreme surface chop. Most rips run out away from shore for only a short distance, then curve and run along shore. If you get caught in a current, don't panic: paddle at a right angle (90°) to the flow, and use its energy to guide yourself to a safe area where you can leave the water. If you must get in through the current, maneuver around the outside of it and enter it from a different direction. Sometimes the currents are narrow streams. It is possible to move a short distance away and be in much less intense waters. Rivermouth and beach breaks usually have strange currents. Steep beaches are another sign of potentially hazardous conditions.

Judgment of wave size is very difficult at some breaks. Surfing has a reputation of only being done in large surf. Sensationalism has fooled the novice surfing enthusiast into thinking that the only wave worth surfing is Pipeline or Waimea Bay. Many people don't realize that the surfers of huge, dangerous waves have spent many years developing abilities and instincts in smaller, safer surf. When you feel proficient in the waves you are riding, try something a bit more difficult. Don't put yourself into the frightening situation of going out in conditions you can't handle. Always take the time to make an accurate assessment of conditions. Once you're out in the water, you're just another object floating in the ocean's realm. Don't risk going out in conditions you can't handle. Underestimating the ocean or overestimating your abilities inevitably results in dire consequences. Most surf spots don't have lifeguards. Surfers have long been regarded as experienced watermen and good swimmers. With the advent of the leash, many surfers have never found a need to develop their swimming skills. Do not depend on anyone to save you in the water. If you get caught in a set of waves, it is almost impossible for someone to get to you.

If you happen to get caught next to some rocks with a wave about to smash you up against them, hold yourself against the rocks. The wave is going to hit you anyway. If you are away from the rocks, you will get hit by the wave, with the force of the wave smashing you into the rocks. By embracing the rocks initially, you'll only get hit by the wave–which should minimize your chance of injury.

You can get an indication of swell size by the number of white water lines between the beach and the breaking wave furthest outside. If there are more than three rows of whitewater between the beach and the wave furthest outside during a set, then it may be too big for beginning.

Larger waves come in sets on a particular day. Sometimes the size difference between the average waves and set waves is minimal, and the waves seem to come non-stop. Other times, the ocean may appear calm. Then, all of a sudden, waves are stacked up ten or twenty deep. Swells coming from different areas and storm systems behave in different ways.

As you surf, pay attention to these details and you will feel more at home in the ocean. The best surfers are usually surprised the least. By learning to recognize the ocean's moods and acting with suitable insight, you can save yourself a great deal of frustration and keep yourself out of unnecessary danger. Any day you go out, watch the sets and time your entry into the water with the completion of a set. That way, you can paddle out without punching through as many waves.

Most surf spots have a take-off zone which is the best area to catch a wave. Always try to catch a wave before it starts breaking. Once a wave starts peeling off, it is more difficult to catch and negotiate. The part of the wave that stands up and breaks first is called the peak.

Taking off at the peak affords the longest and most challenging ride. On a long wall you may be forced to take off down the line because the wave is too difficult to ride from the peak. Take off with as much wall ahead as you feel you can manage. As you get more confident, move further back. Always make sure that you do not take off in front of someone already on the wave, for you can put yourself and someone else in extreme jeopardy.

At some point you may choose to travel for waves. Realize that not everyone is privileged enough to travel in the pursuit of fine surf. Residents often wait through long waveless seasons due to lack of swell, unfavorable winds, or seasonal sand movement. If you do happen to find good waves, be respectful of the local surfers and share with them. If there is a spot nearby which is uncrowded, go there. If there is a beachbreak with peaks up and down for miles in either direction with only two surfers out, don't go out and invade them. Just go and pick a peak of your own. Surfing with a buddy or with a few friends is a very rewarding experience. If crowds are the rule at the spots you surf, be nice and share. "Name" spots are usually crowded, while decent waves nearby go unridden.

Beginning To Surf

Nat Young has put together a great book called *Surfing Fundamentals*. The book contains sequence photos of both basic and advanced surfing maneuvers. His expert insight and experience with the sport will benefit any surfer.

Before you venture out to try and surf waves, try riding whitewater. Find a safe spot where the waves are breaking two or three feet and it isn't crowded. Let the wave break about fifteen feet behind you. The larger waves should break further away from you. Don't go out if the waves are are larger than three feet if you are just beginning.

The whitewater will give you a tremendous push. Paddle as fast as you can before the whitewater reaches you. As in catching waves, you try to match paddling speed to the speed of the incoming whitewater so you can merge with the ocean's energy as smoothly as possible. The earlier you catch the wave, the easier the drop will be to negotiate. Paddle with your weight centered on the board. The tip of the nose should be about two to three inches out of the water. If the tip of the nose is too high, it indicates that you are too far back on the board, and it will be extremely difficult to catch whitewater or waves because you are causing the board to push water, drag and stall. If you are too far forward on the board, the nose will be very low, and most likely it will plow underwater, catch, and flip you head first into the water. This condition is called pearling.

Modern surfboards are very responsive to weight transfer. You can lean forward to catch the wave or whitewater, and then once you have caught it, arch back to shift your weight rearward. Just lay in the centered place on the board and strain forward, or arch back to shift your weight.

Once you are moving and somewhat composed, go from laying to a pushup position, and then right to your feet. It is essential that you master the hands-to-feet takeoff right from the start. If you get into the habit of going to your knees and then to your feet, you will have great difficulty riding a short board in critical waves because you won't be able to get up quickly enough. Shorter boards catch waves later (when the wave is steeper). The steeper the wave is when you catch it, the more critical, quick, and difficult the drop is to negotiate.

Once you are up, try to keep your feet shoulder width apart. You may want to use a wider stance for increased stability. Keep your rear foot about 90° to the stringer, and your front foot about 70° to the stringer.

The stringer should pass under the arch of both your feet. Keep your knees slightly bent and supple so that they can absorb shock. If you don't keep your knees bent and absorb bumps with your legs, you can cause your board to skitter and spin out through turns.

When looking for a spot to surf, don't go out and ride waves that break all at once. These types of waves are called closeouts. The best type of wave for surfing breaks from one side to the other. By the time you are ready to ride waves, you will have developed a preferred stance which will decide which direction is most comfortable for you to go.

The foot which you feel most comfortable putting behind determines whether you are regular or a screw foot. The regular foot puts his/her right foot back near the tail, while the screw or goofy foot puts his/her left foot closest to the tail. Screw foots surf frontside (facing the wave) on lefts (waves that break left to right as viewed from the beach).

Backside refers to surfing with one's back to the wave. A screw foot would be backside on rights, a regular foot backside on lefts. As you can gather from the names, regular foots are more common than screw foots. Some surfers develop the skill of riding frontside on both rights and lefts. This ability is called switch-stance and gives them the advantage of being able to fit into tight tubes of either direction.

You may find yourself having to avoid another surfer or a close-out section in the wave. You can either straighten off and ride the white-water until the wave has calmed, or kick out. Kicking out is accomplished by punching hard on the tail with your rear foot while unweighting your front foot. This weight transfer abruptly turns your board up and over the wave.

Now that we have discussed standing up, we must give equal time to falling off. When you realize a wipeout is inevitable, kick the board away from you and land on your rear-end in the trough of the wave. Keep your head and face covered. In the turmoil of a wipeout, your board or the bottom of the ocean can come up out of nowhere and hit you without warning. Once the turmoil has passed, stay covered until you know where your board is. If you have been driven down deep, open your eyes so that you can swim toward the light. If your board has been pulled toward shore, and you can feel the leash pulling in that direction, you're probably safe. If your leash is slack, there is probably a good chance that your board is very close or outside of you. If your board is outside (closer to the waves than you are) of you, get to it quickly before the next wave pushes it into you. If you can't get to it in time, dive away from your board and try again once the wave passes by. Surfboards propelled by waves can hit very hard, so spend as little time on the wrong side of them as possible. If you loose your board, don't assume it went in. Spot it before you start to swim. Once you have spent time out in the ocean you will inevitably come up against another unnerving situation, the punch-through. Five feet doesn't seem very high when you're standing around. But, when your face is at floor level it is much more imposing. One day while surfing, a larger wave will loom up outside of you and you will be right in its path. Remember, you will not die unless you are in radical 10 foot to 15 foot Hawaiian surf and the circumstances are just right. You may feel as though you're caught in a giant washing machine, and your air supply is running out, but you'll make it. If you see a wave outside of you, and you know you'll never be able to paddle over it before it breaks, just stay where you are. Let the wave break outside of you so that its energy will dissipate before reaching you. If you can't get through it, be as far from the impact zone (where the wave first breaks) as possible.

If you are caught in the impact zone: 1) Make sure there aren't any other surfers near you. If no one is near you, you can shove your board toward shore and dive under the turbulence. 2) If there are others around you, don't let your board go. You can seriously injure or kill someone. Don't get into the habit of depending on your leash. There are several techniques for getting you and your board through waves and whitewater. The first thing to remember is to get your paddling speed up before you encounter the wave. You want to build up as much momentum as possible to get through the wave. As you paddle towards the whitewater, grab the rails of your board (even with your shoulders) and roll upside down while holding the board close with the nose pointed slightly downward. This technique is called turning turtle. Another technique that works well if you're sitting dead in the water with no forward momentum is to grab your board about a foot and a half from the nose, turn it up on a rail and sandwich it under your arm. Hold on to the nose with your other hand as well so it doesn't slide out. Dive through offering as little resistance as possible. If the waves are small, you can simply go into a pushup motion with your arms as the wave hits, forcing the nose under water. The whitewater will then pass between you and your board. The technique I use is the duck dive. It's the best way to maintain momentum as you go through waves so you can get out of the impact zone. Paddle towards the approaching whitewater; at the last second, grab the rails, lean forward and sink the nose down as deep as you can. When you're as deep as you can go by leaning forward, straighten your arms to push the nose down even further. At this point the white water is rolling overhead and your initial penetration is complete. Use one knee to push the tail of your board down (so it's horizontal under water) give a kick with your other leg to maintain forward momentum. As the main turbulence passes lean forward and merge with the rising nose, hang on and you'll be forced out the back and on your way. The duck dive is a complex series of reactions that must be practiced and executed with timing, but it works really well. With experience, you will rely on the technique that best deals with the situation at hand and is most comfortable for you to perform.

It is best to develop a habit of always keeping control of your board. Your board won't be as apt to hit you if you are holding onto it.If you happen to get caught by the first wave of a set you will not have to waste time retrieving your board if you don't throw it away. The time you save may make the difference between getting out or punching through the rest of the waves in the set.

The key to improving your surfing is spending time in the water. If you can, join an amateur surfing organization. Surfing in competition with coaches observing and pacing your progress and strength will help you improve your surfing. Thinking about and acting out what it is you're trying to accomplish is essential to progression. Use video equipment to keep abreast of the hottest surfing and also to critique your own ability. Pushing your ability is going to demand more determination than free surfing. It isn't for everyone so carefully weigh the decision and make sure you're making it for the right reasons.

Through his vast experience in huge surf, veteran surfer Fred Van Dyke has invaluable insight into big wave survival. If you are caught by one of the first waves of a big set, do not dive deep in an attempt to get underneath the energy; instead, let the wave carry you in, away from the impact zone and out of harm's way. By continually diving beneath the energy you tire yourself out and come up for a gulp of air just as the next wave of the set is about to hit you again. If there are more than a few waves in a set, even the strongest of swimmers will become exhausted from repeatedly diving under the waves. Let the first wave hit you and buffet you in, out of the impact zone so successive waves will hit you with less force. This will conserve your energy so you can make it to the channel and back out to the line-up.

When surfing, be considerate of others. Fred Van Dyke relates two well-known rules of experienced surfers: the first man to his feet on the wave has the right-of-way; and never paddle out through the line-up, always paddle around riding surfers. Never cut off a surfer who is already riding a wave. If you are inside and a surfer is riding a wave, don't paddle into his path. Give him room even if it means punching through the whitewater. Always keep the safety of others in mind. Share waves and be humble when riding new breaks. Treat others as you would like to be treated yourself. Leave the problems of land on land. Use the ocean as a paradise to escape everyday life. Appreciate it, and in the ocean you will find a constant source of energy, beauty, and peace.

DESIGN SECTION

I invited shapers from all the top surfboard manufacturers to participate in this Design Section. I asked them to send me their most popular, best performing designs. The only stipulation was that the board should be shaped for a surfer with a height of 5'8" and a weight of 140 lbs. I didn't specify anything else because I wanted them to have total freedom in creating the shapes of their choice. I hope to add designs to this section every time the book is updated, thereby creating a log of surfboard design evolution.

The shapers who created the following boards are some of the best in the business. It's interesting to know how their approaches vary. Shapers who are interested in participating in future design sections can contact me directly for details. For all the craftsmen who contributed boards without which this section could never have gotten started, thanks.

The Design Section for the third edition starts out with quivers from Al Merrick, Rusty Preisendorfer, and Robin Prodanovich. These quivers illustrate design strategy for a wide variety of wave sizes. Tim Bessell, Charley Baldwin, Michael Russo, Matt Kechele, Gary Linden, Gary MacNabb, and Bill Stewart show tri fins that range in length from 5'11" to 6'3". Steve Morgan shaped a 7'0" and Brian Bulkley exhibits the 8'0" gun design he personally refined at huge Pipeline. Eaton's U.E.O. Bonzer design gives us some insight into his continued refinements. I've included a few late model single fins as a reference point.

High performance sailboards started out with surfboard inspired bottom contours. Sailboards enjoyed a rapid design evolution because of the design knowledge, materials, and construction techniques developed for surfboards. The slalom sailboard shaped by Randy French illustrates the specialized bottom contours that have evolved through consistent trial in head-to-head competition. Knowledge gained from experimentation with sailboard design has already started to come full circle, providing insight that will improve surfboard design and performance.

George Orbelian

Design Section Measurement Points

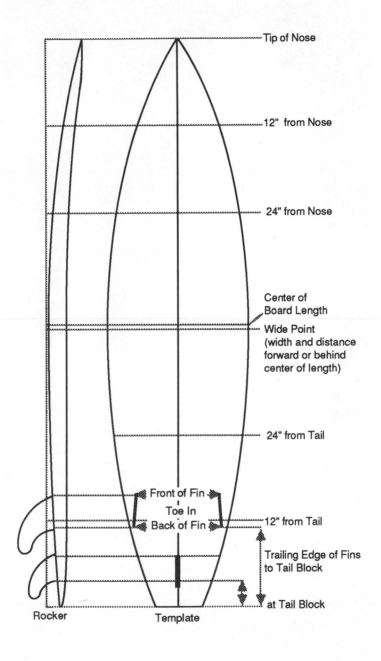

Tip of Nose

12" from Nose

24" from Nose

Center of
Board Length

Wide Point
(width and distance
forward or behind
center of length)

24" from Tail

Front of Fin
Toe In
Back of Fin

12" from Tail

Trailing Edge of Fins
to Tail Block

at Tail Block

Rocker

Template

PRODANOVICH TWIN FIN

SHAPER: ROBIN PRODANOVICH

Tail Design: Single Winged Swallow
Length: 5'10¾"

Type & Layers of Glass
Deck: 6 oz. Volan-2 layers
Bottom: 6 oz. Volan-1 layer

Fin Placement
Measurement from stringer to leading edge of:
Front fin 5¼"

Measurement from stringer to trailing edge of:
Front fin 5¾

Measurement from tip of tail to rear edge of:
Front fin 9¾

Fin dimensions
Base length 5"   Height 5⅞"

[Note: all dimensions are in inches]	Template	Rocker	Thickness	Bottom Contours "V" At Rail
Tip of nose		4⅞		
6" from nose		3¹/₁₆		Flat
1' from nose	13⁵/₁₆	1⅞	1¹¹/₁₆	¹/₁₆
2' from nose	18¾	½	2⁹/₁₆	¹/₁₆
Center	20½	Touching	2¾	⅛
Wide Point	20⁹/₁₆-1¼ behind center			
2' from Tail	19⁹/₁₆	⅛	2⅝	⅛
1' from Tail	16	¾	2⅛	⁵/₁₆
6" from Tail		1³/₁₆		¼
Tip of Tail		2⅛		

Design Comments:

Deck Contours: Flat Deck
Rail Design: Tucked under edge

BREWER FOUR FIN

SHAPER: GARY LINDEN

Tail Design: Double Bump Rounded Square
Length: 5'10"

Type & Layers of Glass
Deck: 5 oz. K Glass–2 layers
Bottom: 5 oz. K Glass–1 layer

Fin Placement
Measurement from stringer to leading edge of:
Front fin 5⅞"   Rear fin: 4⅝"

Measurement from stringer to trailing edge of:
Front fin 6⅛"   Rear fin: 5"

Measurement from tip of tail to rear edge of:
Front fin 12"   Rear fin: 7"

Front fin dimensions
Base length 4¾"   Height 5"

Rear fin dimensions
Base length 3¾"   Height 3¾"

[Note: all dimensions are in inches]	Template	Rocker	Thickness	Bottom Contours "V" At Rail
Tip of nose		5⅛		
6" from nose		3¼		Flat
1' from nose	12⅜	1⅞	1¾	Flat
2' from nose	17¾	7/16	2⅜	1/16
Center	19 7/16	Touching	2½	1/16
Wide Point	19½-3⅜ behind center			
2' from Tail	19	1/16	2 5/16	1/16
1' from Tail	15½	5/16	1 15/16	3/16
6" from Tail		9/16		¼
Tip of Tail		1 1/16		

Design Comments:

Deck Contours: Flat Deck
Rail Design: Tucked under edge-hardest tail area around bumps;
softest around nose.

EATON BONZER

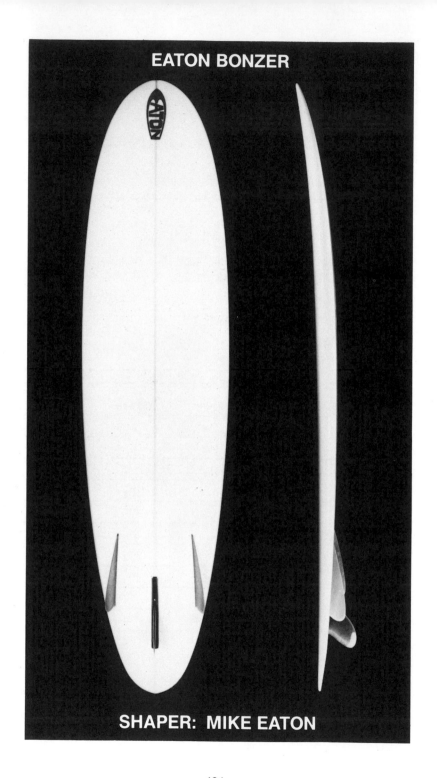

SHAPER: MIKE EATON

Tail Design: Round   Length: 7'6"

Type & Layers of Glass
Deck: 6 oz. Volan−2 layers
Bottom: 6 oz. Volan−1 layer

Fin Placement
Measurement from stringer to leading edge of:
Front fin 5⅜"   Rear fin: on stringer

Measurement from stringer to trailing edge of:
Front fin 6"   Rear fin: on stringer

Measurement from tip of tail to rear edge of:
Front fin 13"   Rear fin: 9"

Front fin dimensions
Base length 10½"   Height 2⅜"

Rear fin dimensions
Base length 5"   Height 4⅜"

[Note: all dimensions are in inches]	Template	Rocker	Thickness	Bottom Contours "V" At Rail
Tip of nose		5½		
6" from nose		3⁹⁄₁₆		¹⁄₁₆
1' from nose	16½	2⅛	2³⁄₁₆	⅛
2' from nose	20	¾	2⅞	³⁄₁₆
Center	21⅛	Touching	3	
Wide Point	21³⁄₁₆-3⅜ ahead of center		3⅛-11 ahead of center	³⁄₁₆
2' from Tail	18³⁄₁₆	½	2⁷⁄₁₆	¹⁄₁₆ "V" at rail ⁵⁄₁₆ - concave
1' from Tail	14³⁄₁₆	⅞	1¹¹⁄₁₆	³⁄₁₆ "V" at rail ⁷⁄₁₆ - concave
6" from Tail		1⁵⁄₁₆		⅜ "V" at rail ⁷⁄₁₆ - concave
Tip of Tail		2		

Design Comments:

Deck Contours: Crowned deck
Rail Design: Soft round rails

GORDON & SMITH TWIN FIN

SHAPER: TERRY GOLDSMITH

Tail Design: Single Winged Swallow
Length: 5'8"

Type & Layers of Glass
Deck: 6 oz. Volan–2 layers
Bottom: 6 oz. Volan–1 layer

Fin Placement
Measurement from stringer to leading edge of:
Front fin 5⅝"

Measurement from stringer to trailing edge of:
Front fin 6⅞"

Measurement from tip of tail to rear edge of:
Front fin 9½"

Fin dimensions
Base length 5"   Height 5⅜"

[Note: all dimensions are in inches]	Template	Rocker	Thickness	Bottom Contours "V" At Rail
Tip of nose		4⅜		
6" from nose		2½		Flat
1' from nose	12⁵/₁₆	1⁷/₁₆	1¹³/₁₆	1/₁₆
2' from nose	17¹⁵/₁₆	¼	2⅝	⅛
Center	19½	Touching	2¾	³/₁₆
Wide Point	19½-2 behind center		2¾	³/₁₆
2' from Tail	18⅞	⅛	2⅝	¼
1' from Tail	15⅝	¾	2³/₁₆	⁵/₁₆
6" from Tail		1¼		⅜
Tip of Tail		2¼		

Design Comments:

Deck Contours: Deck very blended into rails
Rail Design: Tucked under edge - more pronounced in nose and tail area

SEATREND TRI FIN

SHAPER: RANDY FRENCH

Tail Design: Double Winged Rounded Swallow
Length: 5'10"

Type & Layers of Glass
Deck: 6 oz. Volan-2 layers
Bottom: 6 oz. Volan-1 layer

Fin Placement
Measurement from stringer to leading edge of:
Front fin 5¾"   Rear fin: on stringer

Measurement from stringer to trailing edge of:
Front fin 6¼"   Rear fin: on stringer

Measurement from tip of tail to rear edge of:
Front fin 11"   Rear fin: 4¼"

Front fin dimensions
Base length 4½"   Height 4½"

Rear fin dimensions
Base length 4¼"   Height 4½"

[Note: all dimensions are in inches]	Template	Rocker	Thickness	Bottom Contours "V" At Rail
Tip of nose		5		
6" from nose		2⅞		¹/₁₆
1' from nose	12⁷/₁₆	1⅝	2⅛	⅛
2' from nose	17⁵/₁₆	⁵/₁₆	2¾	¹/₁₆
Center	19¹¹/₁₆	Touching	2¾	Flat
Wide Point	19¹¹/₁₆-1¼ behind center		2⅞-4½ ahead of center	
2' from Tail	18¾	¹/₁₆	2½	⅛
1' from Tail	15¹⁵/₁₆	⁵/₁₆	2	³/₁₆
6" from Tail		⅝		⁵/₁₆
Tip of Tail		1¼		

Design Comments:

Deck Contours: Flat Deck - rail turns down quickly
Rail Design: Tucked under edge - rounded nose and swallow points for safety.
Pronounced tucked under edge in area of fins

HOT STUFF FOUR FIN
WAYNE BARTHOLOMEW MODEL

SHAPER: TOM EBERLY

Tail Design: Double Winged Swallow
Length: 5'11"

Type & Layers of Glass
Deck: 6 oz. Volan - 2 layers
Bottom: 6 oz. Volan - 1 layer

Fin Placement
Measurement from stringer to leading edge of:
Front fin 6½"   Rear fin 5½"

Measurement from stringer to trailing edge of:
Front fin 6¾"   Rear fin 4¾"

Measurement from tip of tail to rear edge of:
Front fin 12"   Rear fin 6"

Front fin dimensions
Base length 4¼"   Height 4½"

Rear fin dimensions
Base length 3½"   Height 3½"

[Note: all dimensions are in inches]	Template	Rocker	Thickness	Bottom Contours "V" At Rail
Tip of nose		5⅜		
6" from nose		3⁵/₁₆		1/₁₆
1' from nose	12½	1¹⁵/₁₆	2⅛	1/₁₆
2' from nose	18³/₁₆	½	2¾	1/₁₆
Center	20⅛	Touching	2⅞	1/₁₆
Wide Point 20¼ - 2¾ behind center				
2' from Tail	19½	1/₁₆	2⅝	3/₁₆
1' from Tail	16½	½	1¹¹/₁₆	¼
6" from Tail		⅞		5/₁₆
Tip of Tail		1¾		

Design Comments:

Deck Contours: Flat Deck
Rail Design: Tucked under edge

TOWN & COUNTRY TRI FIN

SHAPER: GLENN MINAMI

Tail Design: Double Bump Swallow
Length: 5'10"

Type & Layers of Glass
Deck: 4 oz. "S" Glass–2 layers
Bottom: 4 oz. "S" Glass–1 layer

Fin Placement
Measurement from stringer to leading edge of:
    Front fin 5¾"   Rear fin: on stringer

Measurement from stringer to trailing edge of:
    Front fin 6¼"   Rear fin: on stringer

Measurement from tip of tail to rear edge of:
    Front fin 11"   Rear fin: 3"

Front fin dimensions
Base length 5½"   Height 4¾"

Rear fin dimensions
Base length 3¼"   Height 3¾"

[Note: all dimensions are in inches]	Template	Rocker	Thickness	Bottom Contours "V" At Rail
Tip of nose		5⅜		
6" from nose		3¼		1/16
1' from nose	12 7/16	1⅞	2	⅛
2' from nose	18⅜	7/16	2 11/16	⅛
Center	20⅜	Touching	2 13/16	⅛
Wide Point	20 7/16-2⅛ behind center			
2' from Tail	19¾	⅛	2⅝	¼
1' from Tail	16⅜	9/16	2 1/16	⅜
6" from Tail		1⅛		⅜
Tip of Tail		2¼		

Design Comments:

Deck Contours: Flat Deck
Rail Design: Tucked under edge - most pronounced in tail/fin area

NECTAR THRUSTER/TRI FIN

SHAPER: GARY MAC NABB

Tail Design: Single Bump Rounded Square
Length: 5'10"

Type & Layers of Glass
Deck: 4 oz. "S" Glass–2 layers
Bottom: 4 oz. "S" Glass–1 layer

Fin Placement
Measurement from stringer to leading edge of:
Front fin 6"   Rear fin: on stringer

Measurement from stringer to trailing edge of:
Front fin 6⁵⁄₁₆"   Rear fin: on stringer

Measurement from tip of tail to rear edge of:
Front fin 11⅜"   Rear fin: 2½"

Front fin dimensions
Base length 4½"   Height 5"

Rear fin dimensions
Base length 4½"   Height 4½"

[Note: all dimensions are in inches]	Template	Rocker	Thickness	Bottom Contours "V" At Rail
Tip of nose		4½		
6" from nose		2¾		Flat
1' from nose	12½	1⁷⁄₁₆	1¹⁵⁄₁₆	¹⁄₁₆
2' from nose	18⁵⁄₁₆	⁵⁄₁₆	2½	¹⁄₁₆
Center	20¹⁄₁₆	Touching	2¹¹⁄₁₆	⅛
Wide Point	20⅛-1⅜ behind center			
2' from Tail	19⁵⁄₁₆	¹⁄₁₆	2½	¼
1' from Tail	15⁵⁄₁₆	½	2	⅜
6" from Tail		1		⅜
Tip of Tail		1⅝		

Design Comments:
Deck Contours: Flat Deck
Rail Design: Tucked under edge - softened towards nose, pronounced under
main standing area/tail

CHANNEL ISLANDS TRI FIN

SHAPER: AL MERRICK

116

Tail Design: Single Bump Rounded Square
Length: 6'2"

Type & Layers of Glass
Deck: 1 layer-4 oz. "S" with 2 staggered deck patches (⅔, ⅓ length)
Bottom: 4 oz. "S"-1 layer

Fin Placement
Measurement from stringer to leading edge of:
    Front fin 5⅜"   Rear fin: on stringer

Measurement from stringer to trailing edge of:
    Front fin 5⅝"   Rear fin: on stringer

Measurement from tip of tail to rear edge of:
    Front fin 10½"   Rear fin: 3½"

Front fin dimensions
Base length 4¾"   Height 4¾"

Rear fin dimensions
Base length 4½"   Height 4½"

[Note: all dimensions are in inches]	Template	Rocker	Thickness	Bottom Contours "V" At Rail
Tip of nose		4⅝		
6" from nose		2⅝		¹⁄₃₂
1' from nose	12⅛	1½	1⅝	¹⁄₁₆
2' from nose	17¹³⁄₁₆"	⁵⁄₁₆	2¼	¹⁄₁₆
Center		Touching	2½	³⁄₃₂
Wide Point	19½ at center			
2' from Tail	18⅝	¼	2¼	⅛
1' from Tail	14⅜	¹³⁄₁₆	1¹¹⁄₁₆	³⁄₁₆
6" from Tail		1³⁄₁₆		³⁄₁₆
Tip of Tail		1¾		

Design Comments:

Deck Contours: Flat deck
Rail Design: Tucked under edge

CHANNEL ISLANDS TRI FIN

SHAPER: AL MERRICK

Tail Design: Single Bump Rounded Pin
Length: 6'6"

Type & Layers of Glass
Deck: 1 layer-4 oz. "S" with staggered deck patches (⅔, ⅓ length)
Bottom: 4 oz. "S"-1 layer

Fin Placement
Measurement from stringer to leading edge of:
    Front fin 5¼"   Rear fin: on stringer

Measurement from stringer to trailing edge of:
    Front fin 5⁹⁄₁₆"   Rear fin: on stringer

Measurement from tip of tail to rear edge of:
    Front fin 10½"   Rear fin: 3½"

Front fin dimensions
Base length 4¾"   Height 4¾"

Rear fin dimensions
Base length 4½"   Height 4½" .

[Note: all dimensions are in inches]	Template	Rocker	Thickness	Bottom Contours "V" At Rail
Tip of nose		5		
6" from nose		3¹⁄₁₆		¹⁄₁₆
1' from nose	11⅝	1¾	1⅝	³⁄₃₂
2' from nose	16¹⁵⁄₁₆	⁷⁄₁₆	2⁵⁄₁₆	³⁄₁₆
Center		Touching	2⁹⁄₁₆	³⁄₁₆
Wide Point	19³⁄₁₆-1¾ behind center			
2' from Tail	18	¼	2⅛	¼
1' from Tail	13⅜	¾	1⅝	¼
6" from Tail		1⅛		¼
Tip of Tail		1¹¹⁄₁₆		

Design Comments:

Deck Contours: Slightly domed
Rail Design: Tucked under edge

CHANNEL ISLANDS TRI FIN

SHAPER: AL MERRICK

Tail Design: Rounded Pin
Length: 7'0"

Type & Layers of Glass
Deck: 1 layer-4 oz. "S" with 2 staggered deck patches (⅔, ⅓ length)
Bottom: 4 oz. "S"-1 layer

Fin Placement
Measurement from stringer to leading edge of:
Front fin 5"   Rear fin: on stringer

Measurement from stringer to trailing edge of:
Front fin 5¼"   Rear fin: on stringer

Measurement from tip of tail to rear edge of:
Front fin 11"   Rear fin: 3"

Front fin dimensions
Base length 4¾"   Height 4¾

Rear fin dimensions
Base length 4½"   Height 4½"

[Note: all dimensions are in inches]	Template	Rocker	Thickness	Bottom Contours "V" At Rail
Tip of nose		5½		
6" from nose		3½		1/32
1' from nose	11¼	2⅛	1½	3/32
2' from nose	16½	⅝	2¼	3/16
Center		Touching	2⅝	5/32
Wide Point	19 at center			
2' from Tail	16¾	⅜	2⅛	3/16
1' from Tail	12⁵⁄₁₆	1	1½	3/16
6" from Tail		1⁷⁄₁₆		3/16
Tip of Tail		2		

Design Comments:
Deck Contours: Flat deck
Rail Design: Tucked under edge

CHANNEL ISLANDS TRI FIN

SHAPER: AL MERRICK

Tail Design: Rounded Pin
Length: 7'6"

Type & Layers of Glass
Deck: 1 layer-4 oz. "S" with 2 staggered deck patches (⅔, ⅓ length)
Bottom: 4 oz. "S"-1 layer

Fin Placement
Measurement from stringer to leading edge of:
Front fin 4¾"   Rear fin: on stringer

Measurement from stringer to trailing edge of:
Front fin 5⅛"   Rear fin: on stringer

Measurement from tip of tail to rear edge of:
Front fin 11"   Rear fin: 3"

Front fin dimensions
Base length 4¾"   Height 4¾"

Rear fin dimensions
Base length 4½"   Height 4½"

[Note: all dimensions are in inches]	Template	Rocker	Thickness	Bottom Contours "V" At Rail
Tip of nose		5⅞		
6" from nose		3¹³/₁₆		1/₃₂
1' from nose	11	2⁷/₁₆	1⁹/₁₆	1/₁₆
2' from nose	16¼	¹³/₁₆	2¼	⅛
Center		Touching	2⅝	³/₁₆
Wide Point	19-2¾ ahead of center			
2' from Tail	16	½	2⅛	³/₁₆
1' from Tail	11½	1⅛	1½	³/₁₆
6" from Tail		1½		³/₁₆
Tip of Tail		2		

Design Comments:
Deck Contours: Flat deck
Rail Design: Tucked under edge

RUSTY SURFBOARDS TRI FIN

SHAPER: RUSTY PREISENDORFER

Tail Design: Double-Bump Rounded Square
Length: 6′2″

Type & Layers of Glass
Deck: 1 layer-4 oz. with 2 staggered deck patches (⅔, ⅓ length)
Bottom: 4 oz.-1 layer

Fin Placement
Measurement from stringer to leading edge of:
Front fin 5½″   Rear fin: on stringer

Measurement from stringer to trailing edge of:
Front fin 5¾″   Rear fin: on stringer

Measurement from tip of tail to rear edge of:
Front fin 10¾″   Rear fin: 3″

Front fin dimensions
Base length 4″   Height 4⅝″

Rear fin dimensions
Base length 4″   Height 4⅝″

[Note: all dimensions are in inches]	Template	Rocker	Thickness	Bottom Contours "V" At Rail
Tip of nose		4⅜		
6″ from nose		2⁹⁄₁₆		¹⁄₁₆
1′ from nose	12	1½	1⅝	¹⁄₁₆
2′ from nose	17⅜	⁵⁄₁₆	2³⁄₁₆	¹⁄₁₆
Center		Touching	2⅜	¹⁄₁₆
Wide Point	19⁵⁄₁₆ - 1 behind center			
2′ from Tail	18¼	³⁄₁₆	2³⁄₁₆	³⁄₁₆
1′ from Tail	14¾	1³⁄₁₆	1¾	³⁄₁₆
6″ from Tail		1¼		³⁄₁₆
Tip of Tail		1¹⁵⁄₁₆		

Design Comments:

Deck Contours: Flat deck
Rail Design: Boxy-tucked under edge

RUSTY SURFBOARDS TRI FIN

SHAPER: RUSTY PREISENDORFER

Tail Design: Single Bump Round
Length: 6'5½"

Type & Layers of Glass
Deck: 1 layer-4 oz. with 2 staggered deck patches (⅔, ⅓ length)
Bottom: 4 oz.-1 layer

Fin Placement
Measurement from stringer to leading edge of:
Front fin 5⅛"   Rear fin: on stringer

Measurement from stringer to trailing edge of:
Front fin 5⁷⁄₁₆"   Rear fin: on stringer

Measurement from tip of tail to rear edge of:
Front fin 11"   Rear fin: 3"

Front fin dimensions
Base length 4"   Height 4¾"

Rear fin dimensions
Base length 4"   Height 4¾"

[Note: all dimensions are in inches]	Template	Rocker	Thickness	Bottom Contours "V" At Rail
Tip of nose		4⅝		
6" from nose		2⅞		¹⁄₃₂
1' from nose	11¼	1¹¹⁄₁₆	1¾	³⁄₃₂
2' from nose	16¾	⅜	2⅜	⅛
Center		Touching	2⁹⁄₁₆	³⁄₁₆
Wide Point	19-1 Behind center			
2' from Tail	17½	¼	2¼	¼
1' from Tail	13⅜	⅞	1¾	¼
6" from Tail		1⁷⁄₁₆		¼
Tip of Tail		2¼		

Design Comments:
Deck Contours: Slightly domed deck
Rail Design: Boxy-tucked under edge

RUSTY SURFBOARDS TRI FIN

SHAPER: RUSTY PREISENDORFER

128

Tail Design: Rounded Pin
Length: 7'0"

Type & Layers of Glass

Deck: 1 layer-4 oz. with 2 staggered deck patches (⅔, ⅓ length)
Bottom: 4 oz.-1 layer

Fin Placement

Measurement from stringer to leading edge of:
Front fin 4⅞" Rear fin: on stringer

Measurement from stringer to trailing edge of:
Front fin 5¹⁄₁₆" Rear fin: on stringer

Measurement from tip of tail to rear edge of:
Front fin 11½" Rear fin: 3½"

Front fin dimensions

Base length 4" Height 4⅝"

Rear fin dimensions

Base length 4" Height 4⅝"

[Note: all dimensions are in inches]	Template	Rocker	Thickness	Bottom Contours "V" At Rail
Tip of nose		5⅜		
6" from nose		3⅜		¹⁄₃₂
1' from nose	10⅞	2¹⁄₁₆	1⅝	¹⁄₁₆
2' from nose	16⁵⁄₁₆	⁹⁄₁₆	2¼	¹⁄₁₆
Center		Touching	2⅝	¹⁄₁₆
Wide Point	18¾ at center			
2' from Tail	16½	⅜	2¼	³⁄₁₆
1' from Tail	12	1¹⁄₁₆	1¾	³⁄₁₆
6" from Tail		1⅝		³⁄₁₆
Tip of Tail		2⅜		

Design Comments:

Deck Contours: Slightly domed
Rail Design: Boxy-tucked under edge

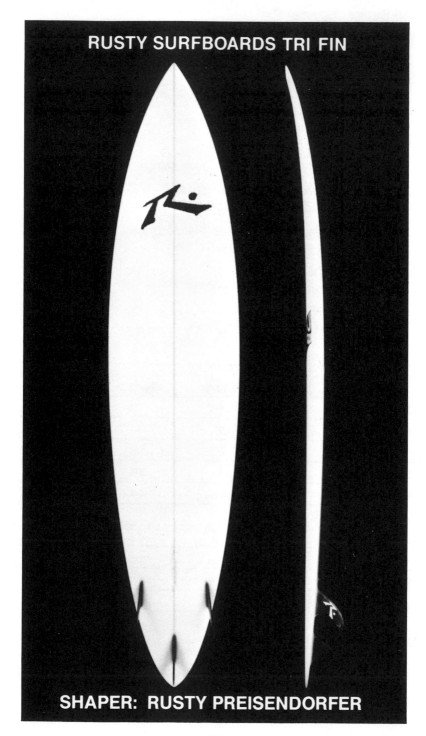

RUSTY SURFBOARDS TRI FIN

SHAPER: RUSTY PREISENDORFER

Tail Design: Pin
Length: 7'8"

Type & Layers of Glass
Deck: 1 layer-4 oz. with 2 staggered deck patches (⅔, ⅓ length)
Bottom: 4 oz.-1 layer

Fin Placement
Measurement from stringer to leading edge of:
Front fin 4⅝"   Rear fin: on stringer

Measurement from stringer to trailing edge of:
Front fin 4¾"   Rear fin: on stringer

Measurement from tip of tail to rear edge of:
Front fin 12"   Rear fin: 4"

Front fin dimensions
Base length 3¾"   Height 4⅜"

Rear fin dimensions
Base length 4¼"   Height 4¾"

[Note: all dimensions are in inches]	Template	Rocker	Thickness	Bottom Contours "V" At Rail
Tip of nose		5¾		
6" from nose		3¾		¹⁄₁₆
1' from nose	10¾	2⁷⁄₁₆	1⅝	³⁄₃₂
2' from nose	16⅛	¹³⁄₁₆	2⁵⁄₁₆	⅛
Center		Touching	2⅝	⅛
Wide Point	18¹³⁄₁₆-2 Ahead of center			
2' from Tail	15½	⅜	2⅛	³⁄₁₆
1' from Tail	11⅛	1¹⁄₁₆	1½	³⁄₁₆
6" from Tail		1⅝		³⁄₁₆
Tip of Tail		2¼		

Design Comments:
Deck Contours: Slighty domed
Rail Design: Boxy-tucked under edge

PRODANOVICH TRI FIN

SHAPER: ROBIN PRODANOVICH

Tail Design: Single Bump Rounded Diamond
Length: 6'2"

Type & Layers of Glass
Deck: 1 layer-4 oz. with 2 staggered deck patches (⅔, ⅓ length)
Bottom: 4 oz.-1 layer

Fin Placement
Measurement from stringer to leading edge of:
Front fin 5"   Rear fin: on stringer

Measurement from stringer to trailing edge of:
Front fin 5½"   Rear fin: on stringer

Measurement from tip of tail to rear edge of:
Front fin 11"   Rear fin: 3"

Front fin dimensions
Base length 4½"   Height 4¾"

Rear fin dimensions
Base length 4½"   Height 4¾"

[Note: all dimensions are in inches]	Template	Rocker	Thickness	Bottom Contours "V" At Rail
Tip of nose		4⅜		
6" from nose		2¾		¹/₁₆
1' from nose	11½	1⅛	1⅝	¹/₁₆
2' from nose	17⅛	⁵/₁₆	2¼	¹/₁₆
Center		Touching	2½	¹/₁₆
Wide Point	19⅜ at center			
2' from Tail	18⁵/₁₆	⁵/₁₆	2⅛	⅛
1' from Tail	14½	1	1¾	¼
6" from Tail		1⅜		³/₁₆
Tip of Tail		2		

Design Comments:
Deck Contours: Flat deck-rail blended onto deck
Rail Design: Boxy rail-tucked under edge

PRODANOVICH TRI FIN

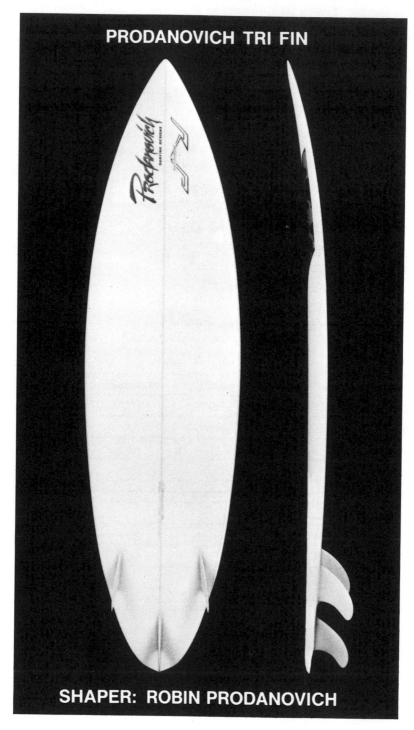

SHAPER: ROBIN PRODANOVICH

Tail Design: Single Bump Rounded Diamond
Length: 6'6"

Type & Layers of Glass
Deck: 1 layer-4 oz. with 2 staggered deck patches (⅔, ⅓ length)
Bottom: 4 oz.-1 layer

Fin Placement
Measurement from stringer to leading edge of:
Front fin 5"   Rear fin: on stringer

Measurement from stringer to trailing edge of:
Front fin 5½"   Rear fin: on stringer

Measurement from tip of tail to rear edge of:
Front fin 11"   Rear fin: 3¼"

Front fin dimensions
Base length 4⅜"   Height 4⅝"

Rear fin dimensions
Base length 4½"   Height 4¾"

[Note: all dimensions are in inches]	Template	Rocker	Thickness	Bottom Contours "V" At Rail
Tip of nose		5		
6" from nose		3¼		¹⁄₁₆
1' from nose	11¼	2	1⅝	⅛
2' from nose	17	½	2³⁄₁₆	⅛
Center		Touching	2½	⅛
Wide Point	19⅝ at center			
2' from Tail	18	⁵⁄₁₆	2¼	³⁄₁₆
1' from Tail	13¾	1	1⅝	¼
6" from Tail		1½		¼
Tip of Tail		2⅛		

Design Comments:

Deck Contours: Domed deck
Rail Design: Boxy-subtle tucked under edge

PRODANOVICH TRI FIN

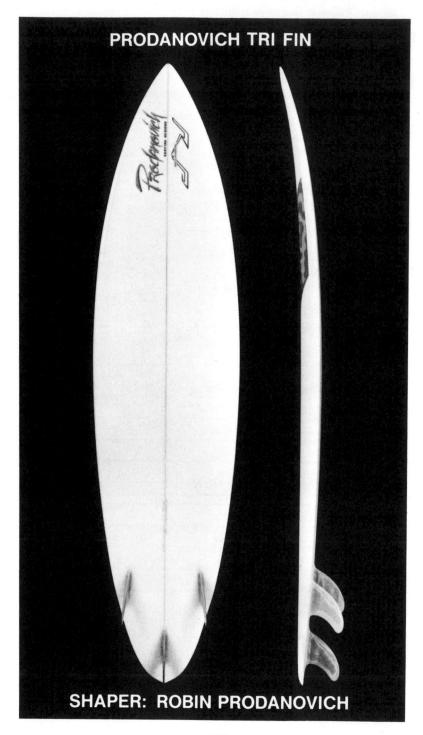

SHAPER: ROBIN PRODANOVICH

Tail Design: Single Bump Rounded Diamond
Length: 7'0"

Type & Layers of Glass
Deck: 1 layer-4 oz. with 2 staggered deck patches (⅔, ⅓ length)
Bottom: 4 oz. - 1 layer

Fin Placement
Measurement from stringer to leading edge of:
Front fin 4½"   Rear fin: on stringer

Measurement from stringer to trailing edge of:
Front fin 4⅞"   Rear fin: on stringer

Measurement from tip of tail to rear edge of:
Front fin 11"   Rear fin: 3"

Front fin dimensions
Base length 4½"   Height 4¾"

Rear fin dimensions
Base length 4½"   Height 4⅝"

[Note: all dimensions are in inches]	Template	Rocker	Thickness	Bottom Contours "V" At Rail
Tip of nose		5⅝		
6" from nose		3¾		1/16
1' from nose	11½	2¼	1¾	⅛
2' from nose	17	⅝	2⁵/16	1/16
Center		Touching	2⁹/16	1/16
Wide Point	19¼-2 Ahead of center			
2' from Tail	16⅞	⅜	2¼	⅛
1' from Tail	12½	1	1⅝	3/16
6" from Tail		1½		¼
Tip of Tail		2		

Design Comments:
Deck Contours: Flat deck
Rail Design: Boxy-subtle tucked under edge

BESSELL TRI FIN

SHAPER: TIM BESSELL

Tail Design: Square
Length: 6'2½"

Type & Layers of Glass
Deck: 4 oz. "E", 4 oz. "S", 4 oz. Stomp patch
Bottom: 4 oz. - 1 layer

Fin Placement
Measurement from stringer to leading edge of:
Front fin 5¾"   Rear fin: on stringer

Measurement from stringer to trailing edge of:
Front fin 6"   Rear fin: on stringer

Measurement from tip of tail to rear edge of:
Front fin 11½"   Rear fin: 3½"

Front fin dimensions
Base length 4⅛"   Height 4⁷⁄₁₆

Rear fin dimensions
Base length 4¼"   Height 4½"

[Note: all dimensions are in inches]	Template	Rocker	Thickness	Bottom Contours "V" At Rail
Tip of nose		5½		
6" from nose		3⁷⁄₁₆		¹⁄₁₆
1' from nose	11⁵⁄₁₆	1¹⁵⁄₁₆	1¾	⅛
2' from nose	17	⅜	2⁷⁄₁₆	⁵⁄₃₂
Center		Touching	2⁹⁄₁₆	⅛
Wide Point	19⅝-3 Behind center			
2' from Tail	18¹¹⁄₁₆	³⁄₁₆	2¼	¼
1' from Tail	14½	⅝	1¾	¼
6" from Tail		1		⁵⁄₁₆"
Tip of Tail		1⅝		

Design Comments:
Deck Contours: Very slightly domed as rail blends onto deck
Rail Design: Subtle tucked under edge

BREWER TRI FIN

SHAPER: STEVE MORGAN

Tail Design: Round
Length: 7'0"

Type & Layers of Glass
Deck: 6 oz. - 1 layer, 4 oz. - 1 layer
Bottom: 4 oz. - 1 layer, 4 oz. tail patch in fin area

Fin Placement
Measurement from stringer to leading edge of:
Front fin 5"   Rear fin: on stringer

Measurement from stringer to trailing edge of:
Front fin 5¼"   Rear fin: on stringer

Measurement from tip of tail to rear edge of:
Front fin 12"   Rear fin: 3¼"

Front fin dimensions
Base length 4⁵⁄₁₆"   Height 4⁹⁄₁₆"

Rear fin dimensions
Base length 4⁵⁄₁₆"   Height 4⁹⁄₁₆"

[Note: all dimensions are in inches]	Template	Rocker	Thickness	Bottom Contours "V" At Rail
Tip of nose		5⁵⁄₁₆		
6" from nose		3⅜		flat
1' from nose	10⅞	1¹⁵⁄₁₆	1¹¹⁄₁₆	¹⁄₁₆
2' from nose	16⅜	⁹⁄₁₆	2⅜	¹⁄₁₆
Center	-	Touching	2¹¹⁄₁₆	⅛
Wide Point	19-1 Behind center			
2' from Tail	17⅛	½	2⅜	¼
1' from Tail	12¹¹⁄₁₆	1¼	1¾	³⁄₁₆
6" from Tail		1¹³⁄₁₆		³⁄₁₆
Tip of Tail		2⅝		

Design Comments:
Deck Contours: Very slightly domed as rail blends into deck
Rail Design: Tucked under edge

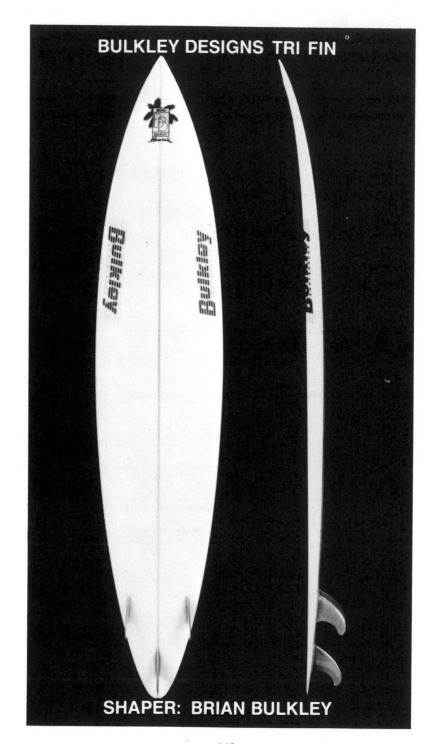

BULKLEY DESIGNS TRI FIN

SHAPER: BRIAN BULKLEY

Tail Design: Round
Length: 8'0"

Type & Layers of Glass
Deck: 4 oz.-l layer, 6 oz.-1 layer
Bottom: 6 oz.-1 layer

Fin Placement
Measurement from stringer to leading edge of:
Front fin 4¹⁄₁₆"   Rear fin: on stringer

Measurement from stringer to trailing edge of:
Front fin 4³⁄₁₆"   Rear fin: on stringer

Measurement from tip of tail to rear edge of:
Front fin 11½"   Rear fin: 3½"

Front fin dimensions
Base length 4"   Height 4½"

Rear fin dimensions
Base length 4"   Height 4½"

[Note: all dimensions are in inches]	Template	Rocker	Thickness	Bottom Contours "V" At Rail
Tip of nose		6⅜		
6" from nose		4¼		¹⁄₃₂
1' from nose	10¼	2¹¹⁄₁₆	1⅝	³⁄₃₂
2' from nose	15¾	¹⁵⁄₁₆	2¼	⅛
Center		Touching	2⅝	³⁄₁₆
Wide Point	18¹¹⁄₁₆-1 Ahead of center			
2' from Tail	15⅛	½	2⅛	¼
1' from Tail	10⁵⁄₁₆	1¼	1½	¼
6" from Tail		1¹³⁄₁₆		¼
Tip of Tail		2⅝		

Design Comments:
Deck Contours: Flat deck
Rail Design: Softened tucked under edge

CB SURFBOARDS TRI FIN

SHAPER: CHARLEY BALDWIN

Tail Design: Single Bump Rounded Square
Length: 6'3"

Type & Layers of Glass
Deck: 6 oz. "S", 4 oz. "S" ⅓ 4 oz. deck patch
Bottom: 4 oz. "S"–1 layer

Fin Placement
Measurement from stringer to leading edge of:
Front fin 5⁹/₁₆"   Rear fin: on stringer

Measurement from stringer to trailing edge of:
Front fin 5¹³/₁₆"   Rear fin: on stringer

Measurement from tip of tail to rear edge of:
Front fin 11"   Rear fin: 3¼"

Front fin dimensions
Base length 4"   Height 4⅝"

Rear fin dimensions
Base length 4"   Height 4⅝"

[Note: all dimensions are in inches]	Template	Rocker	Thickness	Bottom Contours "V" At Rail
Tip of nose		4¹¹/₁₆		
6" from nose		2¹¹/₁₆		¹/₁₆
1' from nose	12	1⁷/₁₆	1⅝	⅛
2' from nose	17¹¹/₁₆	¼	2³/₁₆	⅛
Center		Touching	2⁵/₁₆	⅛
Wide Point	19¹¹/₁₆-1 behind center			Channels extend to 1½ behind center
2' from Tail	18½	³/₁₆	2³/₁₆	⅛ "V" ⅛ channel depth
1' from Tail	14⅞	½	1¹³/₁₆	⁵/₁₆ at rail ³/₃₂ channel depth
6" from Tail		¹³/₁₆"		⁷/₁₆ channels fade out
Tip of Tail		1⁹/₁₆		

Design Comments:
Deck Contours: Slightly domed
Rail Design: Boxy-tucked under edge

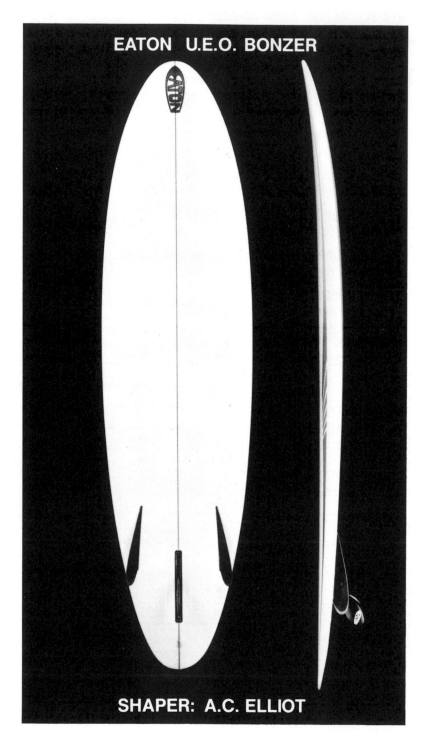

EATON U.E.O. BONZER

SHAPER: A.C. ELLIOT

Tail Design: Round
Length: 7'6"

Type & Layers of Glass
Deck: 6 oz.-2 layers
Bottom: 6 oz.-1 layer with 6 oz. tail patch in fin area
Note: Available with 1½" unidirectional carbon fiber reinforcing
over top and bottom of stringer

Fin Placement
Measurement from stringer to leading edge of:
Front fin 5¼"   Rear fin: on stringer

Measurement from stringer to trailing edge of:
Front fin 6"   Rear fin: on stringer

Measurement from tip of tail to rear edge of:
Front fin 13"   Rear fin: 9¼"

Front fin dimensions
Base length 9¼"   Height 2¾"

Rear fin dimensions
Base length 2½"   Height 5¼"

[Note: all dimensions are in inches]	Template	Rocker	Thickness	Bottom Contours
Tip of nose		6½		
6" from nose		4¼		³⁄₁₆ "V" at rail
1' from nose	15½	2¾	2¼	⁵⁄₁₆ "V" at rail
2' from nose	20	1	3¹⁄₁₆	¼ "V" at rail
Center		Touching	3⅜	
Wide Point	21¾-3½ ahead of center			
2' from Tail	18¾	½	2⁹⁄₁₆	¹⁄₁₆ "V" at rail ⁵⁄₁₆ concave
1' from Tail	14¼	1	1¾	¹⁄₁₆ "V" at rail ½ concave
6" from Tail		1½		¼ "V" at rail ⁷⁄₁₆ concave
Tip of Tail		2½		

Design Comments:
Deck Contours: Domed deck
Rail Design: Soft/subtle tucked under edge

GORDON & SMITH TRI FIN

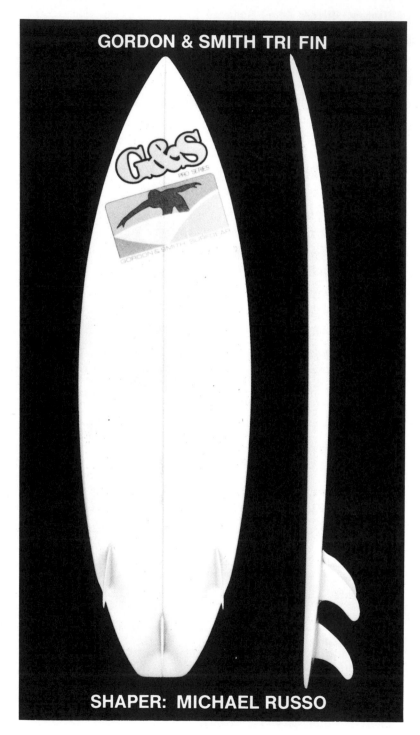

SHAPER: MICHAEL RUSSO

Tail Design: Single Bump Rounded Square
Length: 6'0"

Type & Layers of Glass

Deck: 6 oz.-1 layer, ⅔ length 4 oz., 4 oz. stomp patch
Bottom: 4 oz.-1 layer

Fin Placement

Measurement from stringer to leading edge of:
Front fin 6" Rear fin: on stringer

Measurement from stringer to trailing edge of:
Front fin 6 3/16" Rear fin: on stringer

Measurement from tip of tail to rear edge of:
Front fin 10⅞" Rear fin: 3¼"

Front fin dimensions

Base length 4⅛" Height 4¾"

Rear fin dimensions

Base length 4" Height 4 11/16"

[Note: all dimensions are in inches]	Template	Rocker	Thickness	Bottom Contours "V" At Rail
Tip of nose		4 9/16		
6" from nose		2¾		1/32
1' from nose	12⅛	1½	1¾	1/16
2' from nose	17 13/16	5/16	2⅜	3/32
Center		Touching	2 9/16	⅛
Wide Point	19 13/16-2 Behind center			
2' from Tail	19⅛	3/16	2 7/16	¼
1' from Tail	15⅜	13/16	1 13/16	¼
6" from Tail		1 5/16		⅜
Tip of Tail		2⅛		

Design Comments:

Deck Contours: Slightly domed
Rail Design: Subtle tucked under edge

MATT KECHELE SURFBOARDS TRI FIN

SHAPER: MATT KECHELE

Tail Design: Single Bump Round
Length: 6'1½"

Type & Layers of Glass
Deck: 6 oz.-1 layer, 4 oz.-1 layer
Bottom: 4 oz.-1 layer

Fin Placement
Measurement from stringer to leading edge of:
Front fin 5⅝"   Rear fin: on stringer

Measurement from stringer to trailing edge of:
Front fin 5¹³⁄₁₆"   Rear fin: on stringer

Measurement from tip of tail to rear edge of:
Front fin 10¾"   Rear fin: 3¼"

Front fin dimensions
Base length 4½"   Height 5"

Rear fin dimensions
Base length 4½"   Height 4¾"

[Note: all dimensions are in inches]	Template	Rocker	Thickness	Bottom Contours "V" At Rail
Tip of nose		4¾		
6" from nose		2¹⁵⁄₁₆		¹⁄₁₆
1' from nose	12⅜	1¹¹⁄₁₆	1¾	¹⁄₁₆
2' from nose	17⅝	⁵⁄₁₆	2½	⁵⁄₃₂
Center		Touching	2⅝	³⁄₁₆
Wide Point	19¼ at center			
2' from Tail	18³⁄₁₆	³⁄₁₆	2½	¼
1' from Tail	14⁷⁄₁₆	⅝	2	⁵⁄₁₆
6" from Tail		1¹⁄₁₆		⁵⁄₁₆
Tip of Tail		1⅞		

Design Comments:

Deck Contours: Slightly domed
Rail Design: Boxy-tucked under edge

LINDEN TRI FIN

SHAPER: GARY LINDEN

Tail Design: Rounded Square
Length: 6'1¾"

Type & Layers of Glass
Deck: 6 oz. "E", 4 oz. "E", 4 oz. stomp patch
Bottom: 4 oz. "E"-1 layer

Fin Placement
Measurement from stringer to leading edge of:
Front fin 5⁹⁄₁₆"   Rear fin: on stringer

Measurement from stringer to trailing edge of:
Front fin 6"   Rear fin: on stringer

Measurement from tip of tail to rear edge of:
Front fin 10½"   Rear fin: 3"

Front fin dimensions
Base length 4⅜"   Height 4⅝"

Rear fin dimensions
Base length 4⅛"   Height 4⅜"

[Note: all dimensions are in inches]	Template	Rocker	Thickness	Bottom Contours "V" At Rail
Tip of nose		4⁹⁄₁₆		
6" from nose		2¹¹⁄₁₆		¹⁄₃₂
1' from nose	11¹¹⁄₁₆	1⁹⁄₁₆	1½	¹⁄₁₆
2' from nose	17³⁄₁₆	⁵⁄₁₆	2⅛	¹⁄₁₆
Center		Touching	2⁷⁄₁₆	³⁄₃₂
Wide Point	19⅜-1¾ Behind center			
2' from Tail	18⁷⁄₁₆	¼	2⁵⁄₁₆	⁵⁄₃₂
1' from Tail	15¹⁄₁₆	¹⁵⁄₁₆	1¹³⁄₁₆	³⁄₁₆
6" from Tail		1⁷⁄₁₆		¼
Tip of Tail		2¼		

Design Comments:
Deck Contours: Flat deck
Rail Design: Tucked under edge

NECTAR TRI FIN

SHAPER: GARY MAC NABB

Tail Design: Rounded Pin
Length: 6'3¼"

Type & Layers of Glass
Deck: 4 oz. "E"-1 layer, 4 oz. "S"-1 layer, 4 oz. Butterfly stomp patch
Bottom: 4 oz. "E"-1 layer

Fin Placement
Measurement from stringer to leading edge of:
Front fin 5⁹⁄₁₆"   Rear fin: on stringer

Measurement from stringer to trailing edge of:
Front fin 5⅞"   Rear fin: on stringer

Measurement from tip of tail to rear edge of:
Front fin 10¾"   Rear fin: 3"

Front fin dimensions
Base length 4½"   Height 4⅝"

Rear fin dimensions
Base length 4"   Height 4³⁄₁₆"

[Note: all dimensions are in inches]	Template	Rocker	Thickness	Bottom Contours "V" At Rail
Tip of nose		4⅝		
6" from nose		2¹³⁄₁₆		¹⁄₁₆
1' from nose	11½	1⅝	1⁹⁄₁₆	⅛
2' from nose	17³⁄₁₆	⁵⁄₁₆	2⁵⁄₁₆	³⁄₁₆
Center		Touching	2⅝	³⁄₁₆
Wide Point	19½-1½ Behind center			
2' from Tail	18⁷⁄₁₆	³⁄₁₆	2⁹⁄₁₆	¼
1' from Tail	14⁹⁄₁₆	¾	2¹⁄₁₆	⁵⁄₁₆
6" from Tail		1⁵⁄₁₆		⁵⁄₁₆
Tip of Tail		2³⁄₁₆		

Design Comments:

Deck Contours: Slightly domed
Rail Design: Tucked under edge

STEWART HYDRO HULL TRI FIN

SHAPER: BILL STEWART

Tail Design: Single Bump Rounded Pin
Length: 6'3"

Type & Layers of Glass
Deck: 4 oz.-2 layer, 4 oz. stomp patch
Bottom: 4 oz.-1 layer

Fin Placement
Measurement from stringer to leading edge of:
Front fin 5¾"   Rear fin: on stringer

Measurement from stringer to trailing edge of:
Front fin 6"   Rear fin: on stringer

Measurement from tip of tail to rear edge of:
Front fin 11½"   Rear fin: 3½"

Front fin dimensions
Base length 4¾"   Height 4¾"

Rear fin dimensions
Base length 4½"   Height 4½"

[Note: all dimensions are in inches]	Template	Rocker	Thickness	Bottom Contours
Tip of nose		4⁵⁄₁₆		
6" from nose		2¹¹⁄₁₆		¹⁄₁₆ "V"-½ rail bevel
1' from nose	11⅝	1⅝	1½	⅛ "V"-¾ rail bevel
2' from nose	17⁷⁄₁₆	⅜	2¼	Double concave starts 11" ahead of center ¼ "V"-1" rail bevel
Center		Touching	2⁷⁄₁₆	⅛ "V"-⅞ rail bevel
Wide Point	19⁷⁄₁₆-1¼ behind center			
2' from Tail	18⅜	³⁄₁₆	2³⁄₁₆	¼ "V"-⅜ rail bevel
1' from Tail	14⅝	¹¹⁄₁₆	1¾	Double concave stops at trailing edge of side fins ⅜ "V" (no rail bevel)
6" from Tail		1¹⁄₁₆		⅜ "V"
Tip of Tail		1⅝		

Design Comments:

Deck Contours: Very slightly domed as rail blends onto deck
Rail Design: Specialized double edge chine "hydro" rail used in conjunction with concaves

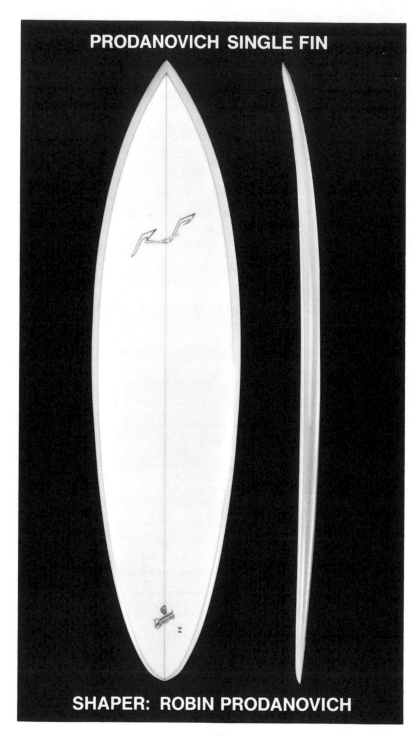

PRODANOVICH SINGLE FIN

SHAPER: ROBIN PRODANOVICH

Tail Design: Rounded Diamond
Length: 6'8"

Type & Layers of Glass
Deck: 1 layer-4 oz. with 2 staggered deck patches (⅔, ⅓ length)
Bottom: 4 oz. 1-layer

Fin style and placement optional

[Note: all dimensions are in inches]	Template	Rocker	Thickness	Bottom Contours "V" At Rail
Tip of nose		5		
6" from nose		3¼		⅛
1' from nose	12¾	1¹⁵⁄₁₆	1⅝	³⁄₁₆
2' from nose	18	½	2¼	³⁄₁₆
Center		Touching	2½	¼
Wide Point	19½-1½ ahead of center			
2' from Tail	17	⁵⁄₁₆	2	¼
1' from Tail	12¾	1	1½	⁵⁄₁₆
6" from Tail		1½		³⁄₁₆
Tip of Tail		2¹⁄₁₆		

Design Comments:

Deck Contours: Flat deck
Rail Design: Boxy-tucked under edge

PRODANOVICH SINGLE FIN

SHAPER: ROBIN PRODANOVICH

Tail Design: Rounded Diamond
Length: 7'0"

Type & Layers of Glass
Deck: 1 layer-4 oz. with 2 staggered deck patches (⅔, ⅓ length)
Bottom: 4 oz.-1 layer

Fin style and placement optional

[Note: all dimensions are in inches]	Template	Rocker	Thickness	Bottom Contours "V" At Rail
Tip of nose		5		
6" from nose		3⁵⁄₁₆		⅛
1' from nose	12¼	2	1⅝	¼
2' from nose	17⅞	⁹⁄₁₆	2¼	¼
Center		Touching	2½	¼
Wide Point	19⅝-3 ahead of center			
2' from Tail	16½	⁵⁄₁₆	2	⁵⁄₁₆
1' from Tail	12	1	1⅜	¼
6" from Tail		1½		³⁄₁₆
Tip of Tail		2³⁄₁₆		

Design Comments:

Deck Contours: Flat deck
Rail Design: Boxy-tucked under edge

SEATREND SLALOM SAILBOARD

SHAPER: RANDY FRENCH

Tail Design: Rounded Pin
Length: 9'3"

Fin style and placement optional

[Note: all dimensions are in inches]	Template	Rocker	Thickness	Bottom Contours
Tip of nose		7¾		
6" from nose	9³⁄₁₆	5⅜	1¹¹⁄₁₆	⁵⁄₃₂ single concave
1' from nose	14	3¾	2⁷⁄₁₆	¼ single concave
2' from nose	19¹³⁄₁₆	1¾	3⁷⁄₁₆	³⁄₁₆ slight double concave
3' from nose	22⅜	¾	4³⁄₁₆	⅛ double concave
Center	22¹⁵⁄₁₆	Touching	4¹³⁄₁₆	⁵⁄₁₆ "V" at rail ³⁄₁₆ concave
Wide Point	22³⁄₁₆-5 ahead of center	¹⁄₁₆	4¾	⅜ at rail ³⁄₁₆ concave
3' from nose	20⅛	⁹⁄₁₆	4⁵⁄₁₆	½ "V" at rail ⅛ concave
2' from Tail	17³⁄₁₆	¾	3⁹⁄₁₆	⁷⁄₁₆ "V" at rail ⅛ concave
1' from Tail	12⅞	1¹⁄₁₆	2⁵⁄₁₆	⁵⁄₁₆ "V" at rail ³⁄₃₂ concave
6" from Tail	9⅜	1⅛	1⁷⁄₁₆	³⁄₁₆ "V" at rail ¹⁄₁₆ concave
Tip of Tail		1³⁄₁₆		

Design Comments:

Deck Contours: Domed deck

Rail Design: Beveled edge on forward rail; hard edge throughout total length of rail

Gordon Clark has made tremendous contributions to the surfboard industry. In addition to developing, improving and supplying the industry with the blanks it depends on, he has written a series of informative brochures. The brochures address various topics of interest to those involved in surfboard and sailboard construction. The following section contains several of Gordon Clark's works, which I felt would be of special interest to the readers of Essential Surfing. The literature contains up-to-date technical information researched by Clark and the top craftsmen he supplies. I want to thank Gordon Clark and the staff at Clark Foam for their help and support.

History of Surfboard and Sailboard Construction

By Gordon Clark

The first known surfboard was recorded by Captain Cook in the 16th century in Hawaii. It was built of koa wood, a native Hawaiian wood similar to mahogany. At the beginning of this century, koa wood boards were still used in Hawaii. They were in a variety of shapes and sizes most of which were in excess of 50 kilos and 4 meters long. In 1905 the sport was introduced to California.

During the 1920's Californians began using redwood to construct boards of a Hawaiian design. By the early 1930's a hollow plywood board was introduced and, later, an Ecuadorian balsa wood and redwood laminated plank with varnish became the most popular board. It was during this period that the first fins were added to the boards for stability. In 1946, the boards were approximately 3.5 meters long and 45 kilos.

In 1946, a California surfer, Bob Simmons, made the first fiberglass covered balsa wood surfboard. This revolutionized the weight, length, and performance of the surfboards. Simmons also built the first polystyrene foam fiberglass surfboards and did considerable development in shapes. In the early 1950's the size of surfboards decreased dramatically, going to a little over 3 meters for the average board. At the same time fiberglassing materials and techniques were undergoing a development use by surfboard manufacturers. Many of the techniques developed during the 1950's are still used in modern surfboard construction.

1958 was the actual beginning of the modern era of surfing. In this year Hobie Alter introduced the first commercially successful polyurethane foam surfboard. While Hobie has since achieved more fame as the developer/designer of the Hobie Cat, which was built using surfboard foam, he remains one of Southern California's pioneer surfboard manufacturers. Due to the fact that foam boards were readily available, lasted longer than balsa wood boards, and offered more advanced designs, the sport of surfing multiplied many times. Much of the early success of the foam surfboard was due to the fact that Hobie's factory developed many of the fiberglassing techniques still used today.

Through 1982 there have been many attempts to construct surfboards using other techniques. Among these are: molded polyurethane boards with fiberglass on the outside, solid honeycomb and honeycomb sandwich boards, polystyrene foam boards, and finally a flexible polyethylene foam board. The only board with any sustained success has been the polyethylene, or flexible surfboard which is primarily a beginner board offering several unique characteristics —flotation and safety.

In periods of extremely high demand, the "pop-out", (as surfer's call them), or molded boards have had limited success when compared to custom surfboard construction. They are heavier and have poor durability. The honeycomb boards have some excellent strength and weight characteristics, but their hollow nature along with their "zipper" effect seam failure after damage, end them in disaster.

Polystyrene foams do not have balanced physical properties and if they are brought up to the durability of a polyurethane board are excessively heavy. For this reason polystyrene foams have not met with commercial success after more than 30 years of research.

From 1955 to 1960 I worked for Hobie, first in glassing, and later in foam. In 1961 I took over the original Hobie Surfboard foam molding factory and formed Clark Foam Products to produce surfboard cores.

After the constrictions of the balsa wood, which was purchased in blocks of a fixed thickness, the freedom to change shape was not apparent to surfboard designers for several years. However, by 1965, foam blank manufacturers had begun making molds to follow design trends. This accelerated the development of new designs and their commercial availability.

The significant changes in modern surfboards have been very subtle. About 1967 Clark Foam introduced the concept of a super light surfboard blank. This was due to enhanced physical properties in our foam formulations. Through the 1970's the quality control of the leading foam manufacturers was the significant breakthrough. In other words, custom surfboard blanks are very difficult to produce, and the refinements in technique and quality control upgraded the product more than base changes in formulation or raw materials.

In 1967 Hoyle Schweitzer built his first Windsurfer out of what is known as the "twelve three" mold. We still have this mold at Clark Foam. Hoyle did his initial development work with us, and in fact, we referred him to fiberglass masts, and assisted him with his other initial developments. At this time, the surfboard industry was experiencing a boom period, and the entire resources of the custom surfboard industry were trying to fill this demand. Due to this fact, Hoyle experienced difficulties in trying to interest anyone to produce his full size sailboards, but he was far sighted enough to see that the market for his windsurfer would grow, and developed the rotational polyethylene process to mass produce a class boat.

Surfboard and sailboard construction diverged at this point. Molded board development in Europe was rapid and represented great innovation and investment. However, in the late 1970's we noted that a few of our larger blanks were going to Hawaii for use in custom sailboard designs. This was unusual for, after years of the molded plastic boards, there was a return to custom fiberglass board techniques. At about that same time, Hoyle returned to us and requested that we develop additional tooling to make a family of large blanks specifically for further development of board shapes. Hoyle was again ahead of his time, for this market was to develop rapidly in Hawaii.

By the 1970's Hawaii had become the center of surfboard design and activity. It has absoutely the best waves in the world and, all good surfers make a pilgrimage to Hawaii as part of their surfing career.

Hawaii also has incredibly good wind and boardsailing/wave riding conditions. It is only natural that the custom industry for board sailing develop there, with many of the top surfboard designers moving to sailboards.

The last year has brought more dramatic changes into the sport of boardsailing, in design and construction, than experienced with surfboard construction during any of its boom periods.

One of the interesting points in surfing has been as the materials improved, the designers/shapers/surfers began working together, and not only did the shape and construction of the surfboards change but the techniques used by the surfer to ride waves changed. To see Hawaiian waves on television, especially Bonzai Pipeline being ridden, was almost inconveivable in 1970. Today it is common place, and there is both equipment and technique which allows almost any expert surfer to ride this treacherous wave - that is, if they have the courage.

Again the designers who made all this possible are centered in Hawaii. There is also significant input from Australia and California. Some of these designers are switching to sailboards, and with the materials and labor supply available, there has been a very rapid evolution in the custom sailboard market creating great enthusiasm and interest. This has resulted in international television coverage of the Hawaiian sailboarders in a comparatively short period of time. It is quite possible that the same thing will happen in Europe for the high wind boards that are coming out of Hawaii now offer performance and technique that is almost unbelievable compared to conventional sailboards.

Materials of Construction

Given any design or shape of a surfboard or sailboard, a decrease in weight will improve performance. This causes a never ending struggle between performance and strength. The strength to weight ratio of a surfboard or sailboard is an important concept in determining which materials and construction techniques to use. It is well understood that boards must have a certain amount of strength, thermal stability, and water resistance to avoid falling apart, filling with water, flex, etc. A balance of properties is very important. For example, you cannot have a very light and strong hollow board with a hole in it, for it will fill with water.

The approach taken with the conventional molded sailboards is to build a board that is impact resistant. For this purpose, the rotational molded or thermoformed plastics have excellent physical properties. If they have a high quality foam core, they will normally resist water absorption and have thermal stability. If they are properly produced they will not bubble or delaminate. In the four-meter range, these boards have, for day to day use, excellent characteristics and are inexpensive to produce.

A surfboard has a much higher skin to core ratio. In other words the surface area of the skin is a great deal larger in relation to cubic volume. Consequently if a modern rotational molded or thermoformed sailboard is built down in the size range of the modern surfboard, which is two to three meters, they are heavy in relation to the custom surfboard. Furthermore, they tend to delaminate under wave riding conditions.

It has been noted, however, that when you build custom surfboards which are the size of conventional molded boards, they approach the weight of conventional sailboards, and are much easier to damage upon impact. The reason for this is that the core of the conventional surfboard (polyurethane foam) is a higher density than that of the molded boards. So, for larger boards, the good points of the conventional molded board are very attractive, while for smaller boards, the conventional surfboard has a higher performance. This is an important point to remember when you consider the future of the high performance, or shorter boards.

There is another factor that has come to bear in Hawaii, and that is that under high wind conditions conventional surfboard construction holds up better in actual sailing than the molded boards. The main reason for this is that the conventional surfboards have higher density foam and a stronger bond between the core and skin, plus the inherent properties of fiberglass.

There are several points in the theory of the modern surfboard that should be elaborated upon for they are the key to their success.

First of all, the modern surfboard blank is molded of a specially formulated polyurethane foam. There are several systems available world wide. Clark Foam uses the only 100% polyester based system. There is one other hybrid polyester-polyether system and several others have reported different types of foam bases other than straight urethane, but basically use the same molding techniques. The key to the success of these boards is the fact that they were formulated over the years for surfboards and are molded in a manner which has proven to provide long durability and ease of fabrication.

When you mold almost any type of low density foam, the outside surface has a thin layer of foam which has fairly poor physical properties. Enhanced physical properties are obtained if this layer is shaved, or planed off. In surfboard type foams, directly under this layer is a layer of high density foam which is much stronger than the foam in the inner core of the blank. For this reason the surfboard blanks are always molded deck down which gives the deck the strongest foam in the entire core. If a mold is not built close to the finished size of the surfboard, the shaper must then shave down into the center core of the blank which consists of lower density and weaker foam. Thus the key to a high strength to weight ratio in a surfboard is the stronger, higher density foam near the surface of the board and a lower density, weaker foam, in the center of the core.

A further advantage in custom surfboard construction is the wooden center stringer. Its function is to keep the two fiberglass skins equal distances apart, thus acting as an "I beam" type stiffener. This fits with common theory that a rigid board is the fastest. Custom boards with stringers are stiffer.

Another attraction of conventional custom surfboard blanks is that they are very easy to shape. The ultimate advantage is that you have a glued, close to shape blank that is both quick and easy to shape and glass, and can either be repeated with relative ease once the shaper has a design which he likes, or can be changed.

Last, fiberglass and foam is easily repaired. There are lots of surfboards still in use which were built prior to the first sailboard!

At present Clark Foam is offered in over 50 shapes for surfboards. Just recently we have made a commitment to follow the sailboard market more closely due to the fact that most of our molds suitable for sailboards have become obsolete with recent design advancements.

Most of our new mold designs are originating in Hawaii. (It also might be interesting to note that Clark Foam supplies literally all the cores for Hawaiian manufacturers, which include such designers as Rick Naish, working with his son Robbie, and Mike Waltze of Sailboards Maui). Also of interest is that Clark Foam supplies, with the exception of Australia, most of the custom surfboard blanks used in the world.

Design

Since the inception of fiberglass/balsa wood surfboards in 1946, the sport of surfing has grown from a few hundred Californians and Hawaiians to a major worldwide sport. During this time the actual techniques used by the surfers while riding waves, the ease of learning, and the incredible performance of modern surfing have evolved.

It seems amazing that sailboards started with surfboard technology, then, for almost a decade diversified into their own technology. At this time it appears that boardsailing has evolved to a point where the developed molded sailboard technology does not achieve the performance of the old custom surfboard technology in high winds. Sailing technique, especially in water starts and jibing, has changed the equipment requirements radically. Consequently, there is a return to surfboard technology for both design and structural reasons.

The bonus of custom surfboard construction is design. It would take the molded board manufacturers a decade to achieve the design results that the custom manufacturers achieved last year. Looking at the history of surfing, my prophecy is that the development of high performance board sailing has just begun.

Analysis of Future Trends
In Surfboard/Sailboard Construction

I. History of Surfboard Construction

Several times in the past it has appeared that a "new" construction-method would change surfboard construction materials overnight. History has shown us, however, that with the exception of urethane foam, no construction material has had an overnight success. Along the same line, due to in-water performance, no semi-rigid surfboard (or sailboard) has ever been able to qualify as anything more than a low cost, or beginners board, from the moment of introduction. Consequently, they will be mostly excluded from this discussion.

*Not an exact date, or the exact date cannot be determined.

The key technological developments in boards which either had a major impact or great potential at the time were:

? - Ancient, solid wood surfboards by Hawaiians. This was carried forward in many sizes, woods, and laminations through the 1950's.

1926 - First use of balsa wood, by Lorrin Thurston of Hawaii.

1929 - Hollow wood board, built and patented by Tom Blake.

1947 - Fiberglass/polyester using balsa wood, first introduced by Bob Simmons.

1950* - First foam board using polystyrene foam and epoxy, by Bob Simmons. Hobie Alter and others built limited numbers of these boards in the 1950's.

1958 - Hobie Surfboards came out with the first fully developed molded urethane blank, "custom" shaped foam board. At the same time, the Hobie factory was using most of the "custom" board glassing techniques still in use today and Hobie had developed the center stringer. Since about 1955, there had been several attempts at urethane, but Hobie was the first to put the entire package together.

1959* - The word "pop-out" was coined as a number of molded (non-shaped), urethane boards appeared on the market. Dave Sweet's "hard-shell" and Chuck Foss's "mat blanks" were the most successful early innovations.

1967* - Carl Pope's epoxy-prepreg-honeycomb hollow "Wave" board was developed and heavily marketed.

1969* - Sailboard "pop-outs" were started. In the United States, this was led by Hoyle Schweitzer at Windsurfer. A urethane core with a thermoplastic skin was used for all initial development. In Europe, this technology exploded.

1970* - The epoxy-polystyrene "custom" built sailboards started to appear in Europe. For the first time, specialized epoxies for surfboard lay-up were developed, along with hot wire shaping techniques.

1983* - It became clear that many major European manufacturers were going to a molded polystyrene core and were beginning to get serious about molded epoxy skins. This was not a new material or construction method, but more a major trend and refinement of a very old concept.

*Not an exact date, or the exact date cannot be determined.

Why Study History?

At this time, there is an explosion of new technologies and materials appearing which may dramatically change surfboard and sailboard construction.

In cloths, we have new fibers, weaves, and even knits. In resins, there are new concepts such as alloys, hybrids, and interpenetrating networks. New ester types, new epoxies, new urethanes, and new foams are appearing all the time.

As history has shown, when new materials appear, there are going to be innovators with the courage and foresight to develop new techniques and use new materials. Also, history has shown us while some innovations will succeed, others will fail.

By now, there is a pretty clear pattern of what works and what does not. This is worth looking at.

Compromise

An Austrailian put a sail on a very short surfboard, took it to Maui and ended the European sailboard maker's massive lead in high performance boards. Why? Europeans had gone overboard for cheapness and durability. They had neglected weight. They called "custom" boards "egg shell" construction and knocked them in the media. Today, they use "custom" epoxy-polystyrene construction for their "World Cup" boards - carefully disguised as "stock" and their paid riders use regular urethane blanks for high wind/wave riding boards. The exact same situation faced the urethane "pop-out" of the 1960's. They emphasized durability and price. A couple of shape changes, lighter weight (and a few other improvements), and they disappeared. On the other side, some manufacturers jumped into Clark Foam ultralights when they first came out with inadequate testing. They fell apart, discrediting everyone involved.

The balance or compromise between properties is extremely delicate. To ignore a single property, even though it appears there is a substantial gain in the other properties, is dangerous. The above example of the indestructible slugs produced in Europe before 1980 is an excellent study of this type of error.

In the examples of specific construction given in the rest of this paper, keep the concept of compromise in mind.

Wooden Era

The ancient Hawaiians evidently tried most sizes, shapes, and had several adequate woods. There was, therefore, no real reason for improvement or choice until 1926 when balsa was first used. By all reasonable logic, balsa, should have dominated surfboard construction after 1926. It was, certainly, intermittently available.

The fact was, however, that balsa was not universally used for about 25 years. In 1929, hollow boards stole the show, followed by redwood and laminated balsa-redwood. There were, in fact, no prevailing methods of construction until balsa-fiberglass came on strong in the early 1950's. The problem shared by both balsa and the hollow board was water absorption. The other big problem with balsa was strength. The comporomise was redwood, which is relatively light, strong, and very waterproof.

Early Foams

Bob Simmons, Hobie, and others dropped polystyrene because of the hassle of epoxy, deterioration, etc. Their reasons were also partly due to the state-of-the-art of glassing to foam. The development of the urethane foam core had the opposite effect. There was an initial acceptance as a "new" thing followed by a wave of acceptance as the maintenance free feature took hold. Then a very strange thing happened. Due to the scramble to get into foam, there were a lot of really weak foams introduced to the market. To compensate for the weak foam, glass was increased and many of the first foam boards outweighed balsa. By todays weight conscious standards, the above fact seems impossible. Switch back to balsa for a few years and you

173

will see why it happened - they soak up water. Within a few years, the "custom board" foams began improving and the old Clark Foam "regular" weight was replaced by the then radical, new "light."

Early "Pop-Outs"

The demand for the new foam boards was tremendous during the first years of urethane foam. The dream of eliminating the traditional shaper, selling the department stores, and getting instantly rich was upon everyone. Dave Sweet perfected the first "no shaping" molded board. For its time, it was probably as good or better than most "customs". Dave's process, the "hard-shell" was, however, extremely difficult and time consuming to manufacture. He kind of burned out. The other "pop-outs" were more or less led by Chuck Foss and his "mat" blank. These were also molded skins with foam poured between them, pre-formed blanks pressed between skins, and even a molded polystyrene core full size board with stiffeners molded inside the foam. A number of "pop-outs" were on the market in the early 1960's and for a time were out-producing the "custom" boards. Several things sealed the fate of early "pop outs". First, they appeared to be super strong. They, unfortunately, were not. They aged very poorly and suffered from delamination and water absorption. The mat blanks especially wicked water and failed in the bond area. Design changes by the "custom" manufacturers did not help. Last, but not least, the "pop-outs" cost of manufacture was higher than expected. As they scrambled to compete, their costs exceeded the costs of a superior, hand-shaped "custom" board and they were doomed. (A prediction that history is maybe repeating itself will be made later in this paper.)

The Ultimate Strength to Weight Board

The highest strength to weight ratio resin/cloth combination is an epoxy "prepreg" which is heat and pressure cured. The highest strength to weight ratio core material is honeycomb. They were introduced as the "WAVE" brand surfboard under the financial backing of the Hexcel (of fiberglass fame) Corporation and none other than SURFER Magazine, who sponsored them to something like a year's free ads (not by choice).

They were apparently doing everything right. Clearly indestructible, at introduction they were something like two pounds lighter than contemporary "customs". The fact that once they were badly dinged they were irreparable seemed to be no problem. The media waited patiently and silently as the water absorption problem of the old Blake hollow boards appeared. An all new "valve" which let air breather in and out but would not let water in was hyped. They filled up with water anyway and faded into probably the largest bankruptcy in California surfboard manufacturing history.

Early Molded Sailboards

The first WINDSURFER was made from the old 12'3" Clark Foam Waimea Gun/Tandum blank. The early developers of the sport desperately wanted a cheaper, automated, high volume, one-design process. The Foss Foam "pop-out" process was next explored. Later, the roto-molded polyethylene-urethane core was developed. This was followed by thermoplastic sheet-urethane core boards. These boards are big, heavy and rely on a very low density core with a thick thermoplastic skin. The skins are actually pretty weak for their weight compared to fiberglass. A large core thickness, however, allows a light but weak form core. Whatever weight saved in the core is put into the skin, plus some, and the boards are really tough. Scale them down to surfboard size, however, and they are very heavy. Scale a surfboard up and it is both lighter and stiffer. Most sailboards are still make using the above construction. Other than being heavy and with an occasional flaw, they are both durable, generally waterproof and dirt cheap to produce. The fact that they are tough to repair does not seem to be a problem as they are equally as tough to damage.

European Devlopment of Epoxy-Polystyrene "Custom" Sailboards

Three key factors were present in the development of polystyrene-epoxy "custom" boards in Europe.

1. There is little wind so very large, thick boards are popular. This puts a premium value on light weight cores as the core weight is significant. (The opposite is true in very small surfboards where the core weight is relatively insignificant). This made the poly-

styrene core "customs" dramatically superior in performance to the thermoplastic-urethane molded boards.

2. Polystyrene was readily available whereas the urethane type surfboard blanks were initially not available. Furthermore sailboarding was relatively unknown at the time so none of the urethane "custom" blank manufacturers were making sailboard size blanks.

3. The small, high performance boards had not been developed.

Aside from several brief attempts at epoxy in California this was the first time epoxy was seriously pursued in "custom" type surfboards. By the end of the decade, resins, hot wire techniques, and supply sources were pretty refined. An American shaper, Gary Seaman, who was designing sailboards in Europe, brought the concept back to California and began promoting polystyrene-epoxy "custom" boards.

In the early 1980's the American and Australian surfboard shapers got involved in the European market primarily due to the revolutionary sailboard designs coming from Hawaii. This introduced conventional urethane blanks to Europe. For some reason many European magazines simultaneously promoted the polystyrene-epoxy. There were numerous articles on do-it-yourself board building using polystyrene and a tremendous light weight comparison. Despite the above the conventional urethane blank has rapidly gained a large share of the European "custom" board market.

European Molded Sailboard Manufacturers Switch to Polystyrene Foam

The European sailboard industry is huge. A relatively few molded board makers have completely dominated the market since the beginning. They have had, however, problems very similar to the surfboard "pop-outs" of the 1960's. Simply put, the "custom" boards are lighter, higher performance, more advanced in design and, in many ways, more durable. As it turns out, in a sport like surfing or sailboarding, no brand wants the image of a "beginner's board." Everyone wants the high performance image. Overnight the leading brands of Europe were being reduced to "beginner's boards" by the "customs". Furthermore the market was stabilizing and there was tremendous over-production of "pop-outs" in Europe. This put pressure on to both improve performance and cut costs. Polystyrene foam did both. It dramatically reduced core weight and at the same time is by far the easiest and cheapest foam to mold. The next step was to switch from thermoplastic to molded epoxy skins. Some manufacturers are attempting this now. What is the future of these recent developments coming from Europe? Historically the pre-molded fiberglass board has had fatal air void/delamination problems, water absorption problems, and a high cost. The polystyrene foam has traditionally wicked up water. Despite the problems of the past, the modern "pop-outs" are better engineered, better promoted, and better distributed than any boards to date. Time alone will be the judge of their worth.

Evolution of the Conventional Modern "Custom" Surfboard Construction

Overall this is a relatively boring story as the changes have been subtle and slow. Molded fins and fin boxes originally developed by Tom Morey were a big change. Foam fins have come and gone several times. Center stringers have gotten simpler with time. About 1966 the concept of having many "close to shape" or as they were known at the time "quick shape" blanks was gradually introduced. This in turn helped to reduce the core wieght by taking advantage of the high density skin inherent in molded urethane blanks. (Incidentally, this was an application of the old Dave Sweet "hard shell" concept). All the time the foam has been gradually improving. There have been, however, no really dramatic overnight changes. It's simply been a little here and a little there. The 1970's saw air-brushing become a part of surfing. It replaced several older art forms including center stringer designs. Air brushing also helped seal the foam affording another slight weight reduction. Shaping has gotten a lot faster due to both the wider selections of molds and the lighter foams. Glassing technique has improved over the years. Resins, cloths, and other materials have been developed which are extremely easy to use, readily available, and reasonable in price.

Major Errors Encountered in Conventional "Custom" Surfboard Construction

Since its inception in 1958 the only serious challenge the hand shaped urethane core surfing board has encountered or faced has been from magazine and media hype which created a temporary demand for other types of board construction. None of these lasted long, so its been pretty much a market in which "custom" boards could get better or worse at will. During the 1960's there were more competing processes and materials than at any other period. One lesson learned in this era was not to cut corners on the foam. There was quite a lively battle and the cheapos pretty much dropped out as consumers wised up. Late in the 1960's, the light weight trend started and never let up to this day. It very quickly cleaned up all the bad craftsmanship associated with heavy boards, but at the same time started a chain of error that goes on to this day. The most common problem has been crushed or delaminated decks - boards get built which are a little too light for contemporary materials. (Some of this is due more to over-shaping than to materials). Browning and patches of water induced foam damage has constantly plagued the urethane foam. Another key contemporary problem has been that both resins and cloths have usually been chosen for looks and ease of application. Sadly, the 1960 Hobie had a tight, stiff, flat weave cloth and a high solids isophtalic polyester resin. The average 1985 board has a twist (or partial twist) weave and an almost half styrene, thin, cheap ortho resin. The consequence is that "customs" would have been a lot stronger (and maybe lighter) if more emphasis had been spent on strength. Last, there has been a bigger than ever push in the last few years for lighter weight. This has triggered a demand for lighter foam. The lighter foams, with no significant changes in glassing materials, has brought forth a large number of very weak boards. Last, the lower density foams have been taxing the current state of the art urethane "blank" molding process to its limits.

II. Analysis of History

A Study of Periods of Conflicting Materials

The wooden surfboard era through 1950, the early foam surfboard period, and the contemporary molded sailboard/"custom" sailboard represent periods where no definite material dominated. We still do not know what will happen with sailboards, but surfboards are clearly history.

Looking back to wooden boards, it seems a miracle that the light weight balsa was so slow catching on. It was available in California where it was used on movie sets. Later it was imported specifically for surfboards. It was fairly accepted laminated with redwood, but rather late in the period. Even after fiberglass there was no rush to balsa (in part because the early fiberglass/resins were so crude.) A dilemma was that the hollow board was also a strong contender - especially in Hawaii.

What was happening? Well, the hollow boards were light and cheap but took in water. (This will be covered in detail later). Redwood was too heavy, but okay in all other respects. Other woods, including spruce, were no match for redwood and were pretty phased out by 1950 with the exception of Koa and other local woods in Hawaii. Balsa was, despite all the modern boat building literature, a sponge and had a serious maintenance factor. By about 1950, however, fiberglass/polyester got to the point that balsa could be strengthened and protected. At that point, it briefly took over only to be replaced by urethane foam in 1958.

When foam took over, it cost more to manufacture, was in many ways weaker, and all but the initial Hobie's weighed as much or more than the average weight balsa. The initial years were plagued by massive delamination problems, expansion and contraction, discoloration, and in some of the "pop-out's," water absorption. The overriding sales point was "maintenance free." For the first time, you could ding your board and not have to race to the beach, dry it and patch it. There was, however, an incredible difference in foam boards. The hype was on. Trade shows had one manufacturere hitting a board with a 2"x4", the early magazine ads were full of wild claims, and the buying public became confused. (Finally, the better manufacturers threatened to boycott the magazines unless they started cleaning up the false claims). This was a period of real confusion primarily because the "pop-out's" were both selling cheap and physically strong. Another confusing point was that some of the so called "custom" boards had inferior foam, glass, and craftsmanship to the "pop-outs."

By the late 1960's, the buying public had wised up. The "pop-out" branded the surfer as a beginner or a fool. (By then, it was common knowledge that some molded boards were a bad value.)

Shape and appearance changes also struck hard on the "pop-outs" and cheap foams. Shape changes increased their tooling costs and made their inventories obsolete. A final blow was probably the trend of the higher quality manufacturers to "clear" boards. This showed the foam and all flaws. The buyers were really wising up.

Beginning in 1969, there was a rapid depression in surfboard sales. By the time this came, there were virtually none of the huge foam "pop-out" manufacturers left. By the end of the slow years, most of the low end "custom" board builders and lower quality foam molders were gone. When all the advertising and boom-boom was over, the public went for the high end "custom" construction and there has been no substantial change to this day.

Sailboards are currently in a period of conflicting materials. Pick up a sailboard magazine and you will see confusion equal or surpassing the heyday of competing surfboard construction techniques. After reading the ads, look at product (if you can find it). Then tear into some of the boards. The best boards are master pieces of engineering and design. The worst of the molded are pure junk. The most incredible feature of many molded boards is the low wholesale cost. (This is often the result of the high dollar, over capacity, etc., rather than good engineering.) When we put the conventional "custom" board up against the molded boards we have the old "ding proof" feature. Other points are that some of the low quality urethane cores delaminate and the latest light weight polystyrene cores are going to be very vulnerable to water absorption and deterioration. To top things off a lot of the boards are heavy and shapes are obsolete.

Predicting the Future from History

History to date has conclusively shown the following features to be critical in a successful board.

1. STIFFNESS: Only a very low performance board such as a beginner's board or a surfboard for very small, mushy waves can be flexible. This is evidenced by the failure of Morey-Doyle surfboard, some of the stringerless boards of the 1960's and the recent race by molded sailboards to become stiffer. Since stiffness has a weight penalty, it is clear from the past that weight will be compromised for stiffness.

2. IMPACT STRENGTH: In high performance boards impact strength has not been a particularly important feature. The only important material which was fairly rejected in part due to impact strength was balsa prior to the use of fiberglass. The molded sailboard

makers stressed impact strength and were probably dismayed when "custom" boards grabbed the high performance end of the market. Some of the old "pop-out" surfboards featured very high impact strength, but failed to sell. The honeycomb epoxy "WAVE" board was stronger on impact than any surfboard or sailboard to date and was very hard to scratch. "Custom" surfboards have been sacrificing impact strength for both weight and cosmetic value (by use of low end but clear resins) for years. Probably the best way to sum up this strength feature is to state that impact strength must be maintained at a level which allows the board to be damage-free under normal, reasonably careful service. If very light weight products are involved, impact strength will usually be compromised by light weight. If total entry level, or media educated customers are involved, impact strength may be very important.

3. DENTING, DELAMINATION, AND OTHER STRUCTURAL WEAK-NESS: Balsa was the first material to encounter denting type deterioration. Its lack of acceptance for almost 25 years is partially explained by denting even though it's weight was far superior to other materials. "Custom" surfboards have been plagued with dents, especially where knees or feet are placed. The denting could always have been stopped by an addition in weight. Also, stronger resins and cloths help stop denting. Again, this has not been done, evidently because it is not considered that important. In the case of contemporary surfboards, almost all boards are prone to dent.

The next structural problem, delamination, is the all time eliminator of board manufacturers. Early hollow wood boards had delamination problems. Balsa semi-delaminates when moisture gets to the wood. The "pop-out" of the 1960's suffered severe delamination problems. Early foams for "custom" boards, especially the weaker brands of the 1960's, suffered from some delamination. Molded sailboards have been plagued with delamination.

Many of the above examples of delamination represent boards which almost never dent on impact but instead delaminate. "Custom" boards normally delaminate only due to impact. Many of the "pop-out" boards have delaminated due to thermal shock, bending, "gassing", etc. Most minor delaminations of "custom" boards can be repaired. Molded boards which delaminate are normally finished. The most severe example was the all epoxy-honeycomb

"WAVE" board. Once it started to delaminate, it went so fast the term "zipper" was coined to describe the phenomenon.

The mechanics of delamination has often been misunderstood. In a totally closed cell foam and sealed skin, a small bubble, heated by sunlight, will cause a tremendous pressure on the foam-glass bond. A porous bonding agent, such as the old fiberglass "mat" blanks, wicked water causing water deterioration followed by delamination. Some adhesive systems for molded boards have also allowed water deterioration. Also a simple ding in any board will bring in moisture through the surface hole and damage foam cells which causes deterioration followed by delamination. Simply heating and cooling even causes some strain on the foam-skin bond. This caused a rash of "show-room" delaminations in the 1960's primarily attributed to weak foam.

It is a fact that most of the "pop-outs" of the 1960's went out of business primarily due to delamination and that it is probably the most severe problem that has faced the molded sailboard industry.

Other structural failures can be from a variety of causes. In "custom" surfboards they usually represent a bad blank, glassing, or application technique error.

In sum, history has shown us that limited denting has been tolerated. Delamination is usually the death blow to a board or even an entire construction material and/or technique. Other structural flaws have been varied over the years and probably not worthy of discussion.

4. ENVIRONMENTAL DETERIORATION: Wet balsa wood tends to rot or deteriorate. Some of the lower price brands of the early urethane foams deteriorated slightly in the presence of salt water. Some also tended to expand or contract in direct sunlight. All urethane foams brown in direct sunlight or in the presence of water. The common polystyrene foams melt at a relatively low temperature. In fact, they melt close to those temperatures occasionally encountered by surfboards. They are also attacked by a number of weak solvents including gasoline. Also, occasionally a brand of molded board has a serious urethane foam deterioration problem. Both epoxy and polyester resins have given excellent environmental service. The thermoplastic skins used for molded sailboards have occasionally failed in very high temperatures. In fact, this has been rather common. In sum, however, the thermoplastics are well suited for

the surfboard/sailboard environment. The general conclusion is that cores are the traditional environmental problem, with the focus generally being on the core-skin interface.

5. WATER ABSORPTION: In 1953, the author of this article, then a teenager, got his very first job in the surfboard industry. The employer was the legendary Tom Blake, inventor of the hollow surfboard (and the fin for that matter). The job was to repair a rather large Waikiki Beach fleet of rental surfboards. The job was divided into two parts. First a group of hollow boards were given layers of fiberglass tape around the seams to reseal the seams. The second part was to strip the glass off a bunch of water-logged balsa boards, dry them, lightly re-shape down to virgin wood, and re-glass the boards. Tom explained the entire surfboard water absorption problem as follows: "The hollow board must have a plug to both drain the water and keep the air pressure the same inside the board as outside. In a board without leaks or holes the plug has to be removed after surfing or the air inside would get hot and blow the board up until a seam ruptures. Inserting the plug into a hot board and then cooling it causes a vacuum inside the board which can suck the deck and bottom inward. Usually the boards have very small leaks which are difficult to find and fix. For that reason it is a good idea to take the plug in and out several times after entering cold water. This relieves the vacuum and helps keep out the water." The basic point is that all boards are at one time or another heated very hot by sun or radiant heat. Then they are thrown in cold water creating a tremendous suction as the gas (or air) within the board cools. This applies to hollowboards, wood boards, and foam boards. The above mentioned Waikiki balsa rental boards were examples of this sucking action. Under heavy use, they experienced the traditional balsa problem and sucked water into the wood along the bond line between the resin and balsa. The same sucking problem explains in part why balsa, the first (and still somewhat competitive in weight) light weight core material laid around for almost a quarter of a century before it was accepted. Simply put, it was a real maintenance problem before fiberglass.

The next really serious attempt at hollow boards was the epoxy/honeycomb "WAVE" board. It was really sealed up tight. Without a breather, it would collapse or blow up. No matter what was tried, water eventually got in. Amazingly, some of it even got into the hollow honeycomb cells.

It would appear the above thoroughly describes the sucking phenomenon in boards. It does not for there are more subtle ramifications. Probably the first example that came up after the urethane foam boards were introduced was that the "pop-out" and even some very early "customs" made from very poor quality foam started delaminating. Water was discovered between the foam and the skin. This phenomenon was very evident in the "mat" blanks which were prone to open cell foam, etc., near the surface of the blank. This water in turn caused the foam to deteriorate and triggered the delamination. (As a note, plastic foams used in boards to date have all tended to experience some form of deterioration in the presence of water.) Many types of molded sailboards have experienced the above type water absorption and/or delamination. It is often not important, however, because their thick skin and heavy weight cover up the problem. Two products which are normally billed as "water-proof" are balsa core for boats and polystyrene foam. Many boats are built with balsa and manufacturers claim there is negligible water absorption. Put balsa under water and these claims are somewhat disproven. In a surfboard, however, balsa rapidly soaks up water. Common polystyrene foam is widely used as flotation. It works very well as a swimming pool kick board, etc., even though it is a fairly porous material. Pull a vacuum on it while surrounded by water, and it's porosity shows up for it loads up with water. The most extreme example of the suction phenomenon can be seen in a well used board made from CLARK FOAM. There are often brown patches near small dings or almost invisible holes. This represents moisture that has been sucked into the damaged area and often causes more damage by attacking the good foam.

These brown spots deserve some further discussion: Early urethane foams, including CLARK FOAM, were very prone to brown spots, or limited water absorption and deterioration. This problem in CLARK FOAM will always be limited to a small area around the ding. In the new lighter blanks, however, it requires drying and a patch much sooner. The main point here is that the increase in brown spotting with the lighter foam may be an omen that there is a weight limit in even urethane foams due to the suction problem in surfboards.

The European inspired use of polystyrene foam for both "custom" and molded sailboards, and recently surfboards, has re-opened the problem of water absorption. The workable solutions go back to 1929. Either (1) make the board 100% water tight or, (2) thoroughly cool the board to a temperature lower than water temperature prior to entering the water. This causes an expansion rather than a contraction of the gases inside the board as it warms up.

Today, we find the molded boards using polystyrene have a pretty good seal due to the nature of the coverings used. "Customs" take more care and attention.

Recently, it was reported that pre-pressuring might solve the suction problem. It is doubtful, however, that this will work since air is difficult to contain and distribute in a thin skin board - especially if it is already dinged.

Last, some evaluation is necessary based upon the amount of use the board receives. The reality is that many boards, and especially the cheaper boards, are rarely put in the water. For these boards, almost anything will work.

Consequently, it is fairly conclusive to assume that the hot board/cold water problem is conclusively solved only by a non-porous core and adhesive.

6. BOND STRENGTH BETWEEN CORE AND SKIN: This is one of the great and often over-looked strengths of the so called "custom" or hand lay-up boards. All molded and most "pop-out" boards to date have had to rely on a pressure-type adhesive or foam in place bond. These processes also must work blind as there is little hope of thorough inspection without destroying the board. Great strides have been made in this area in recent years. The risk, however, is still present. In a hand lay-up there is no risk. For molded boards using an adhesive for bond, there is an additonal weight factor. In any board a good bond is mandatory.

7. DESIGN OR SHAPE CHANGES: This has been going on since the inception of surfing and has quickly spread to sailboards via the "customs". There is no way it is going to change and recent plastics journals indicate the large molded board manufacturers are rapidly acquiring the technology to change designs both inex-pensively and rapidly.

III. CONCLUSIONS

The conventional urethane core "custom" surfboard construction method is still going to remain the dominant *high performance* construction method for the foreseeable future. There could, however, be a lot more pressure on the conventional "custom" boards as the result of:

1. Molded sailboards are improving at a rapid rate. They are privy to the latest developments in plastics technology. At the same time, "custom" board makers are at the bottom end of the technology ladder and usually dependent on a handful of relatively small distributors, manufacturers, etc., for technical advancement. Furthermore many of the molded board makers are justifiably paranoid about "custom" boards. The molders can therefore be expected to focus their development and other energy on the customer who is attracted to a high performance board.

2. Polystyrene foam, despite its shortcomings, is clearly recognized as the lightest weight sailboard and surfboard core material. In very large boards it creates such a significant weight savings that it is more or less mandatory in competition. The weight factor alone will create a demand for these products. There will also be some strong divisions among both molded and "custom" manufacturers as they battle for sales by advocating either urethane or polystyrene. This has already started as there are both molded and "custom" manufacturers who express a total commitment to polystyrene.

3. The conventional surfboard and sailboard media, either through direct advertising or by editorial, traditionally has had great power to influence customer demand. As a matter of good business practice the media tends to support its advertising customers or who it believes are its future customers. Also their resources are not really great enough to afford fully qualified writers and editors for all articles. Should the media either accidentally or deliberately promote one of the newer technologies there could be a tremendous impact on the conventional "custom" board market. (Incidentally this has happened quite often in surfboards. Examples were some of the "pop-outs", the "WAVE", and the flexible boards which

probably would have had negligble sales without massive help from the media.)

4. The current over-valuation of the dollar and some government subsidies make the cost of products more dependent on the country they were produced in rather than the efficiency of the process. This clearly hurts a large part of the "custom" board industry.

IV. NEW TECHNOLOGIES

There are two basic types of plastics - thermosets and thermo-formed. Thermosets are a two or more component resin system which mixes together and irrevocably cross-links. Thermoformed plastics melt upon heating and solidify at ambient temperatures. They can later be re-melted and re-formed. The above definition applies to most products, however there are some hybrids which more or less use both methods simultaneously.

Using the above definitions it seems simpler to approach this discussion by separating the categories into thermoset and thermo-formed foams and resins. Fabric will be kept separate.

Thermoset Foams

Urethane is the word which encompasses most thermoset foams. This includes some of the PVC "hybrids" and the so called "phenolic" surfboard blank. Outside of the urethane category there are some very promising high strength foams but unfortunately they do not lend themselves to surfboard construction. Within pure urethanes, the development has been painfully slow as most of the basic chemistry and materials are fairly old. There could, however, always be a dramatic breakthrough. This would probably come in the form of an all new polymer. A serious problem confronting molded thermoset foams for "custom" boards is that in the process of producing the lighter blanks it is getting very difficult to:

1. Weigh the smaller amounts of resin components accurately.
2. Hand pour or distribute the smaller quantities of resins.
3. Achieve the "blow" necessary to fill the mold.
4. Eliminate "pour-lines" or "late close" marks and other flaws in the lighter blanks.

In other words, even with a higher strength to weight ratio foam, there appears to be a mechanical limit to the weight of the thermoset blank.

In molded boards the urethane technology is fairly developed. The lack of need for a cosmetic and shapeable foam leaves this field far more flexible for improvements than "custom" boards. Should the cheaper, easier to mold, and lighter polystyrene foams suffer their predictable water absorption and deterioration problems it would be expected that there will be more development in urethanes in this area.

Last it is fairly certain that there will be strength increase and cell size reduction in CLARK FOAM in 1985. This will in effect absorb less resin and produce lighter boards. At the same time there will, however, be strength ramifications due to the decrease of resin absorbed into the foam.

Thermoformed Foams

All thermoformed foams are made by mixing a blowing agent into the plastic which expands it. In the making of a continuous bun or slab process (such as polyethylene foam used in body boards) a prohibitive expense is involved. The process is so complicated, it is doubtful this technology will be used to mold a large part in the foreseeable future. Of the slab type processes, there are some very high strength to weight ratio foams available. They have, however, all been looked at and rejected for good cause. This could change but nothing appears forthcoming at this time.

The "bead" technique is used to make the polystyrene foam commonly found in sailboards and surfboards. It is sold as small pellets or "beads" of polystyrene encapsulating a heat activated blowing agent. Upon application of heat, the polystyrene melts and a gas is released blowing the bead up. The beads fuse together and upon cooling form a very high strength to weight foam.

Polystyrene "bead" foam has two great advantages. It is dirt cheap and it is very easy to mold. Consequently it was highly developed many years ago and the common grades are high volume, commodity plastics. Recently, it has been announced that several others types of plastics may be made in "bead" (or equivalent) form, either now or in the future. This could have a profound effect on board construction as the newer plastics would undoubtedly offer some properties which are superior to polystyrene. The foremost of these would be higher temperature, solvent and water resistance. Among other things this could open polyester resins to lighter foams.

One development that could be expected in thermoformed foams is that an inexpensive commercial hot wire will be developed for "custom" manufacturers. This would take advantage of the way "bead" foams are distributed. To save freight, they are shipped in "bead" form and blown into buns by local molders. There are literally hundreds of such operations around the world and the prices are very competitive. (The above answers the question "Is CLARK FOAM going to get involved?"). Another development that could be expected with any significant volume in thermoformed foams is that blanks will be molded 100% to shape. Unlike urethanes or thermosets, this is extremely easy with "beads". Shapes can be very intricate, close tolerances can be held and there are almost zero rejects. The latest technology in this field is reported to be vacuum assisted molding which allow almost unlimited weight reductions.

Thermoset Resins

Polyesters will probably continue to be the work-horse of the "custom" board industry. The standard "surfboard" resins will probably not get stronger unless they are threatened by a switch to epoxy or some other higher strength resin. Epoxies are also well developed. They are, however, easily modified and have hardly been explored by the "custom" board industry, so there is probably a lot to learn. Problems that are not going to disappear in epoxies are their cost and nastiness. In between the two extremes of polyester and epoxy there is an incredible range of new development. Some of the most exciting new work is in alloys, hybrids, and inter-penetrating networks (or two dissimilar resins reacted together.) The above work holds the potential to exceed the physicals of all known resins. There are also still a lot of old and new polyester type resins which have hardly been looked at by the surfboard industry. They offer the potential of improved strength without the cost and problems of epoxy.

Thermoformed Resins

These are the skins used by most of the molded sailboard industry. Here expect all state-of-the-art changes to appear over-night, because the molded board makers are on top of things. One factor which could hold back some materials is price. They are already spending way too much on their high performance boards and are probably quite alarmed as the costs of "custom" boards are starting to look good. This is the same trend we saw in "pop-out" surfboards. They actually ended up costing more than "customs".

Fibers

At least one new fiber of the Kevlar type with claimed improvements has been announced. Carbon fiber is still dropping in price and appearing in more hybrid weaves. Expect it to appear in surfboard type cloths more and more. There is a new "knit" rather than a "weave" cloth. It is still at the 10 ounce level at this time. It has the types of physicals that offers optimum performance for boards.

Stiffeners

The "I-beam" or center stringer concept is still the highest strength to weight ratio technique. Pre-impregnated, uni-directional fiber glass on the top and bottom of the stringers may prove to enhance stiffness in boards. Despite the extreme rigidity of uni-directional carbon fiber, it is highly unlikely that the thinner boards will ever be stiff enough without a stringer.

New Manufacturing Technology

It seems that every craftsman, mechanic, designer, or engineer who has become involved in surfing or sailing has thought about a better board. There has been no lack of ideas, or for that matter, people eager to quit their job and go into the board making business. Consequently, it is safe to assume that advanced state-of-the-art materials and manufacturing techniques are available to the board industry.

At this point, it appears that to develop anything truly revolutionary, a tremendous amount of money must be spent. There seems to be a lack of incentive to do this because:

1. You can buy fairly good, molded board factories for a fraction of their cost.

2. The companies with the capitol for huge investments, like Bic, Coleman, and AMF, have purchased going factories and evidently are not pushing for new technology. These are the types of firms that love to invest ten million dollars on a new process if it will make an end product which is profitable and dominates the market.

3. There are still a large number of proponents of class racing in sailboards. This holds back development.

4. In surfboards, there is a tremendous labor force for making "custom" boards. These boards peform far better than molded surfboards. They are also inexpensive.

5. It appears that "custom" sailboards are gaining a market share in Europe, Japan, and the United States. The "custom" board is, and has always been, labor intensive, and requires little capitol for equipment. (Automation of the "custom" process has been advanced by a few "custom" manufacturers. This includes computer controlled shaping machines.)

6. The leading molded sailboard manufacturers appear to be using the latest plastics molding technology. In other words, they are throwing their best shots at this time.

Surfboard/Sailboard Stringer
Stiffness and Breaking Strength

We have done some limited development work and testing of stringers for the purpose of assisting customers interested in special performance boards.

While stringer design has been discussed with us by many board builders over the years we would like to note that for many years George Downing of Hawaii has been concerned with surfboards breaking in half in big surf and very recently Ed Angulo of Hawaii was kind enough to inform us of the fact that higher performance racing sailboards work better if the board is very stiff.

Before proceeding we wish to emphasize that our work has been very limited and does not address a very wide range of materials, construction techniques or testing methods. As a matter of fact, with the exception of a carbon fiber tape, we used standard surfboard materials and with the exception of one center strip/glass combination, the stiffners were all of fairly common design.

In drawing your own conclusions of our work please keep in mind that weight is the usual penalty for strength. With the development of carbon fiber we should probably add that money may be the penalty for stiffness. We cannot resist this opportunity to again remind everyone that there are a number of stronger materials available for building surfboards and sailboards. They are, however, hard to find, hard to use, more expensive, and often look awful!

Last we should mention that in the water lots of strange things can happen. Boards often break where theoretically they should not. It is quite possible that a flexible or rubber effect could absorb and at the same time deflect a lot of impact forces. There could be a resonance or vibration effect. For sure there is a fatigue factor.

Theory and Analysis of Stiffness and Strength

The stiffness and breaking strength of a surfboard is made up of a combination of components.

The strength of the foam, the stringer(s), and the glue by themselves are components of the final stiffness and breaking strength, which are best measured in the shaped blank. Since the shaped blank is very weak, even with lots of wood stringers, it is fairly obvious the final stiffness and breaking strength has little to do with the foam and stringers standing alone.

The fiberglass alone obviously has little strength. Also a board with glass on one side only is quite weak.

At this point we conclude that the majority of a surfboard's stiffness and/or breaking strength comes from:

1. The "sandwich construction" effect of two fiberglass "skins" separated by a foam "core". ("Skins" and "core" are the standard engineering terms for "sandwich construction".)

2. The "I-Beam" effect of two fiberglass "flanges" separated by a wood stringer "web". ("Flanges" and "web" are the standard engineering terms for "I-Beams".)

The basic theory of "sandwich" or "I-Beam" construction is that the "core" or "web" holds the "skins" or "flanges" the same distance apart. This means that to bend, one "skin" or "flange" must stretch and/or the other "skin" or "flange" must compress.

Since the "skin" or if you wish, "flange", of a surfboard is fiberglass which is very strong it is extremely difficult to bend or break the surfboard by stretching or compressing the fiberglass "skin."

There is a great deal of information available for "sandwich" and "I-Beam" construction including detailed mathematical models which will calculate the bending of such structures under specific loads. From the mathematical models we feel three things are especially significant in designing a stiff or strong surfboard. They are:

1. The "core" or "web" thickness (or simply the surfboard thickness) is by far the most important factor in stiffness and strength.

2. The "core" or "web" must hold the skins apart the same distance or it will contribute to the bending. In other words, a weak or flexible foam or stringer will result in a flexible board.

3. The "skin" or "flange" strength.

Observations

Throughout the literature on "sandwich" and "I-Beam" construction "buckling" of the compressed "skin" or "flange" is discussed as a common point of failure. In surfboard construction, theory suggests that compression "buckling" would be the point of failure when a surfboard breaks in half. Experience and our testing has verified this as true. The exact sequence of events appears to be that the compression induced "buckling" causes a delamination between the foam and glass followed by the glass breaking. (Or in some cases massive delaminations). After the compression side lets go there is normally some crushing of the foam on the tension side as the glass is compressed against the foam. Last, if the breaking force continues, the tension side of the glass breaks.

Another observation we feel is key in the design of stiff boards is that stringerless boards are extemely flexible. The difference in flexibility between an unshaped stringerless and a shaped stringer board is far less dramatic than the differences between the two boards when glassed. In other words, the stinger has a dramatic contribution which is not at all obvious in a shaped blank.

Since it will not be tested we would like to emphasize Item 1 above, the importance of board thickness, with our observations of the Hobie "Phil Edwards Model" of the 1960's. It was one of the all time break in half surfboards! The construction was three spruce stringers, one ¾" (19mm) and two ¼" (6mm), double 10 ounce cloth, around 10 feet (3M) long, wide and extremely thin. It gave the impression of incredible strength. They broke with a predictable frequency while comparable boards with thicker construction had no problems.

Our Conclusions from Theory and Observations

The obvious factors in stiffness and breaking strength of surfboards is the glass/resin stiffness strength and thickness, the foam density (or strength) and the stringers.

A factor often overlooked but extemely significant is the board thickness.

The most subtle point, which we feel is dramatically brought out by the stringerless board, is that the stiffness comes more from the "I-Beam" effect of the stringer holding the glass above and below it equal distance apart and less from the foam which is obviously flexing a little and not holding the glass equal distances apart.

Last, both a stiff skin and/or a strong fiberglass to foam bond are the determining factors in the final breaking strength of a surfboard.

Testing

The following were chosen as sample to be tested as they gave a wide variety of theoretical combinations:

1. An ⅛" (3.2 mm) spruce stringer glued normally.
2. An ⅛" (3.2 mm) spruce stringer with one layer of 8 ounce cloth on each side of the stringer. (In other words, a glass-spruce-glass "T-Band").
3. An ⅛" spruce stringer with two ⅝" x .010" uni-directional carbon fiber tapes slightly overlapped under the glass, both above and below the stringer. (The carbon fiber was laid in place just before the glass cloth was set in place).
4. An ⅛" (3.2 mm) spruce stringer was glued normally. Next a vibrating "saber saw" with a short, thin blade was run along both sides of the stinger on the "top" or "deck" side of the sample. Then two strips of common 8 ounce weight by 3" (7.6 cm) fiberglass tape was laid in the saw holes about half way and bent over into an "L" shape on the "deck". The final glass was put on top of this and the resin applied. The same procedure was then applied on the bottom. (It should be noted that the "saber saw" worked very well but there was a "gassing" problem with the resin during the lay-up).

Our sample preparation procedure was to select similar spruce and use a single block of foam of dimensions 4" (10.1 cm) x 2' (61 cm) x 8' (244 cm). The four stringers, including the one with fiberglass on each side, were glued with Koppers surfboard grade laminating resin. The entire block was then milled to 3½" (8.9 cm). The carbon fiber and tape were put in place (after sawing) and a single layer of 8 ounce cloth was laid up using carefully weighed and mixed Koppers surfboard grade laminating resin. The entire block was then heat cured for over 48 hours at about 135 degrees F (57.2 C). The sample was then cut into uniform 6" (15.2 cm) strips.

To test the deflection and breaking point the samples were placed between stands 90" (228.6 cm) apart, and fifty pound (22.7 kg) bags placed on the samples in the center.

It should also be noted that the size of the sample was meant to be a compromise between surfboards and large windsurfers. Therefore the weights are not really conclusive and makes direct weight comparisons of the four type samples difficult.

Our General Conclusions

To begin with the fiberglass-wood-fiberglass stringer proved to be almost identical to the plain wood stringer!

This is extremely consistent with "I-Beam" theory where the "webs" only function is to hold the two "flanges" an equal distance apart under loading!

Meanwhile for a negligible or inclusive gain in stiffness and breaking strength, we gained .542 pounds (246 g). Essentially this leads us to the conclusion that standard wood center strips are very adequate. It should also cast doubts on the popular theory that a stronger stringer will make the board stiffer and stronger!

The carbon fiber uni-directional tape brought a highly positive result for the high performance sailboards. It was light, a .443 pound (201 g) gain. It clearly exhibited the most stiffness with light loading. (In the test results up to about 25% of it's breaking strength). It was clearly superior in stiffness to 1 and 2 in heavy loading.

More than anything the carbon fiber result indicates to us that strong materials are important.

It also again indicated that the standard wood center stringer was adequate since the carbon fiber would not have worked if the stringer was not holding the "skins" or "flanges" the same distance apart.

The interesting point was the breaking strength of the carbon fiber board. It was almost identical to the stock and fiberglass stringers! It explains the reason for the frustration experienced by many big wave board builders who have used "uni-directional" cloth to build "unbreakable" boards which broke anyway. The reason for this is that the "buckling" forces are dependent on the foam-glass bond which the "uni-directional" cloth did not help.

The most outstanding part of Sample 4 is that it had twice the breaking strength of the standard surfboard construction!

The disadvantage was that it weighted 2.49 pounds (1128 g). Upon close examination, however, the weight would have been less in a surfboard due to the contour. (For that matter, so would the fiberglass-wood-fiberglass stringer weight). The essential key to Sample 4's strength was that the bond between the outside fiberglass and the foam was extremely strong. Consequently it took a tremendous force to "buckle" or delaminate the fiberglass from the foam and begin the break.

Our conclusions from the tests could be summarized as follows:

1. The basic wood stringer is adequate for keeping the two fiberglass skins equal distance apart.
2. There is little or no gain by wider or reinforced stringers.
3. More stringers, spread out uniformly over the thicker sections of the board should help the board's stiffness but will not necessarily help the (bond dependent) breaking strength.
4. Exotic or high strength cloth/resins help the board's stiffness a great deal. These materials are, however, far more efficient for enhancing stiffness when placed right over a stringer. (Again they do little for the breaking strength).
5. The ultimate breaking strength is (normally) a function of the resistance to buckling on the compression side of the board's bending. This strength is extremely dependent on the foam-fiberglass bond. A board's breaking strength is also influenced by a stiff fiberglass "skin" which helps distribute the forces trying to break the foam-fiberglass bond over a larger area.

Our Recommendations for Building Very Light, Stiff Boards

1. Go as thick as possible.
2. To keep weight low use as light a cloth as possible for surface areas.
3. Treat each stringer as an "I-Beam". Use uni-directional cloth and, if you can afford it, carbon fiber tape right over the stringers. Count on these "I-Beams" to support the balance of the board which may be kept weak to keep the weight down.
4. Go to several stringers spaced a few inches apart and constructed like item 3 above if you need more stiffness.
5. Should you be using a low density blank, keep the "I-Beam" type "flanges" as narrow as possible as the foam will not help hold the "flanges" a constant distance apart.
6. Use the strongest materials available.

**Our Recommendations for Building Very Light Boards
Which Will be Difficult to Break in Half**

1. Go as thick as possible.
2. Assume that any break will start in the glass right over the stringer on the compression side of the bending force by breaking the foam bond. Reinforce this area by both:

   a. Thicker-stronger laminate.

   b. Enhance the bond to the stringer and surrounding foam. (The technique we used in Sample 4 is one idea but undoubtedly we went too deep alongside the stringer).
3. Use several stringers with the above reinforcement to increase the breaking strength.
4. Use a heavy density blank for better bond strength and "buckling" resistance.
5. Use the strongest materials available.

Average Weight of Wood Stringers
(Clark Foam Products Test Method)

Purpose

To illustrate the amount of weight added by stringers to the total blank weight, a series of experiments were conducted on each of the wood types available in blanks.

Method

Ten stringers of each type wood available as stringers were carefully precut to the shape of an unshaped blank. The stringers were weighed individually, and their respective weights recorded. These weights were then averaged.

Results

Wood Type	Board Size	Stringer Thickness	Weight In Grams	Weight In Pounds
Paper	6'9"	—	15.650	.03lb./.48oz.
Balsa	6'9"	*3/32	68.600	.15lb./2.4oz.
Basswood	6'9"	1/32	86.000	.18lb./3.0oz.
Redwood	6'9"	*3/32	145.450	.32lb./5.0oz.
Magnolia	6'9"	1/16	150.920	.33lb./5.2oz.
Spruce	6'9"	*3/32	165.750	.36lb./5.7oz.
Butternut	6'9"	1/8	166.125	.36lb./5.7oz.
Basswood	6'9"	*3/32	170.500	.37lb./5.9oz.

Conclusion

The weight of the wood stringer will be further reduced by approximately 3% after shaping.

*NOTE: 3/32" is referred to as 1/8" on price list and when ordering. For full 1/8" stringers, please specify "full" or "exact" 1/8".

Gerisch Products, Inc. has put together an information booklet called "Projects with Fiberglass and Resins." I was impressed with the booklet and asked for permission to present the sections most applicable to surfboards in *Essential Surfing*. I want to thank Gerisch Products, Inc. and their General Manager, Robert Pettijohn for their contribution.

How to Fiberglass A Surfboard

Supply Check List

1. *2 - T-bar Racks* which suspend the blank during construction. Make these by standing a 44" long 2" x 4" in a 5 gallon bucket full of sand. Nail a nine-inch piece of 1" x 2" flatwise to the top of the 2" x 4". Wrap the ends of the 1" x 2"s with several feet of masking tape or some flexible foam to prevent scratching of the surfboard during construction.

2. *Surfboard Blank* - shaped to your liking. Made from *polyurethane* type foam.

3. *Resins* - Laminating Resin - 1 gallon
   Sanding Resin - 2 quarts
   Finishing Resin - 1 quart
   (Including sufficient catalyst / hardener)
   Note: The amounts of resin shown are most likely in excess of what would actually be used to make one board. Available package sizing was considered.

4. *Cloth* - surfboard quality, *silane* finish, 27" - 30" wide, 4, 6 or 7½ oz. wt. - Enough to cover the length of your blank three times.

5. *Fiberglass fin rope.* ½" diameter - approx. 18" for one fin.

6. *Surfboard Fin(s)*

7. *Masking Tape* - 2"

8. *Brush,* bare handle, natural bristle, 4" wide

9. *Scissors*

10. *Utility Knife* or single edge razor blade

11. *Mixing Sticks*

12. *4 - 2½ qt. paper buckets*

13. *Sandpaper* - 60 D and 100 C, alum. oxide
    400 A and 600 A, Wet or Dry, silicon carbide

14. *Surform*

15. *Heavy Duty Buffing Compound*

16. *Nu Glass Fiberglass Polish*

17. *Clean Polish Rags*

18. *Hand Cleaner Bio-Seven Resin Cleaner*

19. *Acetone Solvent* (For tool cleanup)
20. *Tarpaper* - or other protective floor cover
21. *Safety Glasses, Gloves, Protective Clothing, Dust Mask and Respirator*
22. *Clean Water* - An instant supply in case of chemical eye contact.

Optional

23. *Opaque Pigments*
24. *Fiberglass Decals*
25. *Vibrator Sander or disc sander* with foam back-up pad
26. *Buffer - Buffing Pad*

How to Fiberglass a Surfboard

1. Place the blank on the rack with the deck (topside) facing up. Apply two or three layers of overlapped 2" masking tape - 1" inside the rails (outer edges) of the blank. Be sure the outside edge of the tape makes good contact with the blank, but leave the inside edge loose. This tape will catch resin runs during lamination.

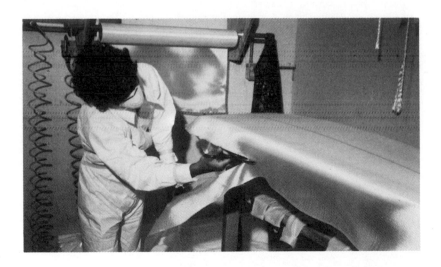

2. Turn the blank over (bottom up). Lay out a piece of cloth over the blank with 3 inches of excess on each end. Carefully trim the sides of the piece, leaving enough excess to lap about 1" over the masking tape on the underneath side. Save the scrap pieces.

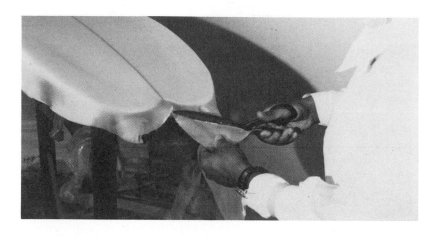

3. V-notch the tail and nose section, so the cloth does not buckle when you lap it underneath.

4. The first lamination will require about 1½ qts. of laminating resin. If a colored board is desired add opaque pigment. If you want a clear board with a decal, fold back the cloth and pour a little catalyzed resin on the decal location. Put the decal in place, and gently work out any air bubbles with a squeegee. Replace the cloth.

5. Pour some catalyzed resin on the center of the board.

6. Use the squeegee to spread the resin and completely wet the cloth. Add more resin as required, working it outward towards the nose, tail and rails.

7. Bring resin over the rails, to completely saturate the overhanging cloth. Squeegee excess resin out of the cloth creating a smooth, neat laminate.

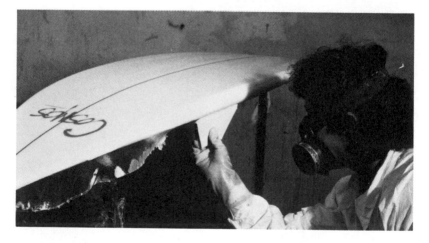

8. When the overhanging cloth is completely wet, lap it underneath, over the masking tape with your squeegee. Start at the mid-section and work towards both ends. Check the entire laminate carefully before it gels. Remove any trapped air bubbles with your squeegee or gloved finger tips. Add more catalyzed resin to dry areas and smooth them out. Clean your squeegee in acetone before the resin gels. If any buckles develop along the rails, snip the cloth vertically up through the buckle and dovetail the section.

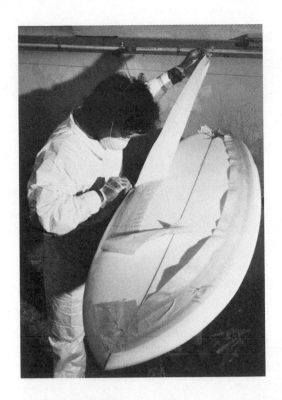

9. Check the lamination frequently as the cure progresses. When the resin reaches a semi-hard stage, turn the board over and knife trim the laminate along the edge of the masking tape. Try not to cut into the foam, but be sure to sever the laminate completely. Slowly peel away the masking tape and excess laminate, checking for uncut glass strands as you pull up the tape.

10. Prepare for the deck lamination by first cutting a "deck patch," a piece of cloth extending from near the tail about two-thirds the distance towards the nose. Trim the deck patch at the rail line as neatly as possible.

11. Cut and trim another full length piece as you did for the bottom side, leaving the same amount of excess for lapping around the rails. V-notch the tail and nose as before.

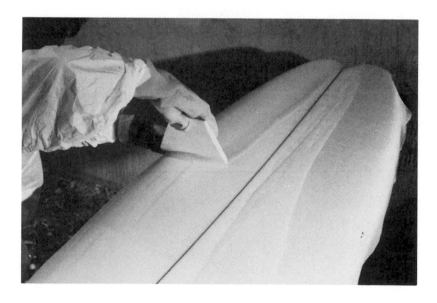

12. This time there is no need to apply masking tape to the other side. Center the deck patch under the full length cloth piece. Catalyze 1½ qts. of laminating resin and laminate the deck just as you did the bottom side.

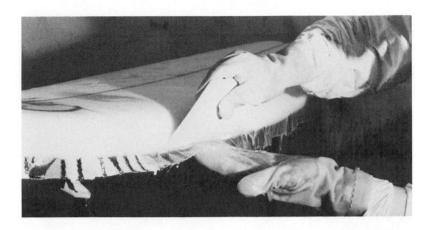

13. When the cloth hanging over the rails is fully wet, lap it around the rails onto the bottom side laminate. Again, begin this process at the middle of the board and work towards the nose and tail.

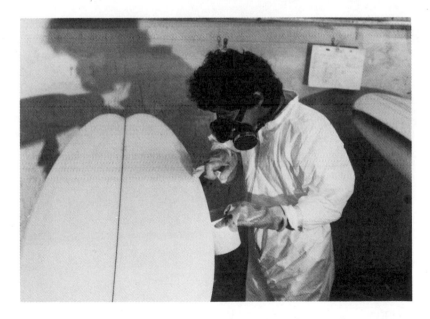

14. Check the entire laminate carefully before gel. Remove air bubbles and fill in dry spots. Clean your squeegee in acetone before the resin gels. After the resin cures surform down any remaining projecting fiberglass or air blisters.

15. Keep the deckside up. Prepare for the sanding resin application by applying masking tape around the entire rail edge. Carefully adhere to top edge of the tape to the rail, but allow the bottom half to hang free. When the sanding resin coat is applied, the excess resin will flow over the tape and drip off onto the floor instead of running around to the bottom side.

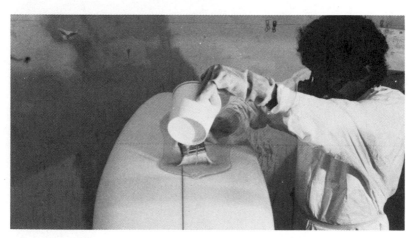

16. Catalyze one quart of sanding resin. Adjust the catalyst percentage for a fast gel (12 to 15 minutes) to prevent excess resin drainage. Pour about one-half the resin on the middle of the board and spread it over the entire board using long, light pressured brush strokes. Work the resin outward towards the rails allowing the excess to flow over the masking tape and to drip onto the floor.

17. Early in the application some of the excess resin can be caught in the mixing bucket and re-applied to resin-lean areas, but this should not be tried when gel time is approaching. Use crosswise strokes once during the application, but finish with a series of long, light strokes the full length of the board. Clean your brush in acetone before the resin gels. Remove the masking tape after the resin gels.

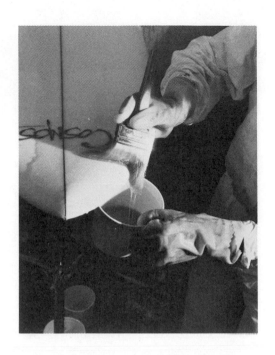

18. After the resin cures, turn the board over, bottom side up. Apply masking tape to the rails as you did previously.

19. Prepare to mount the tail fin or fins by first holding them in position with masking tape as shown in this photo. This board will have four fins, but one, two, or three fins can be attached. A single fin would be applied at the center of the blank, about six and one half inches from the tail.

20. Catalyze a small portion of laminating resin and flow some along the base of the fin on each side. Use a mixing stick to apply the resin. When the resin gels remove the masking tape.

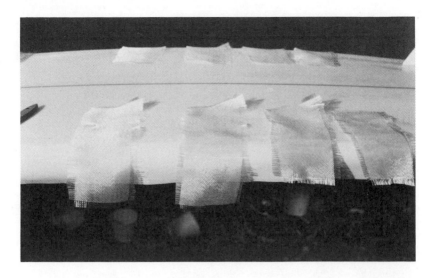

21. Using your left-over scrap cloth, cut four pieces for each tail fin. The pieces should be about three inches wide and two inches longer than the base of the fin.

22. Saturate a section of ½" fiberglass fin rope in a pint of catalyzed laminating resin.

23. Partially squeegee out the excess resin with your gloved hand.

24. Gently lay the saturated rope against the base of the fin and cut it leaving an extra inch of rope extending from both sides of the fin base. Apply rope to both sides of the fin. Gently press the pieces together at both ends.

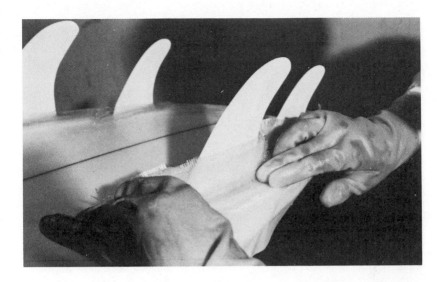

25. & 26. Center two pre-cut cloth pieces over each saturated rope piece allowing one-half of the cloth width to contact the fin and the other half to sweep down over the surfboard. Using your brush, gently remove the trapped air and excess resin from the cloth and the saturated rope beneath, forming a smooth fillet on both sides of the fin base. Do not trim the excess cloth at this time. Allow the fins to set firmly.

27. Apply a full coat of sanding resin to the entire bottomside. Brush a full coat over the fin(s). Brush the resin lengthwise and then crosswise. Excess resin will run off the tape you applied earlier.

28. As before, the final strokes should be applied lengthwise with very light pressure on the brush. Remove the masking tape after the resin gels. Allow the resin to cure before proceeding.

29. thru 34. Begin the sanding process by carefully hand sanding the excess fiberglass from the fin(s) and smoothing the fin base. Use 60 D grit alum. oxide sandpaper over the entire surface first, then switch to 100C alum. oxide paper. Be sure to sand down the remaining ridge on the rails where the masking tape was pulled and feather out the cloth overlap on the bottom of the board. If you have power equipment such as a vibrator sander or disc sander, it will speed up the sanding process, but be extremely cautious about cutting into the fiberglass cloth. If you use a disc sander, we strongly recommend also using a soft foam back-up pad. Be very particular about the care you apply at this phase of the job, because it will greatly influence the final strength and appearance of your board.

30. 31

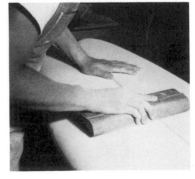

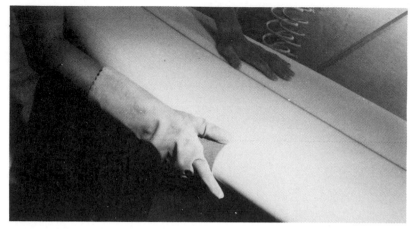

32.

33.

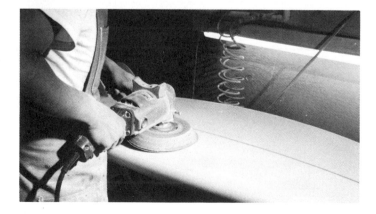

34.

35. When the entire board is smoothed to your satisfaction with 100C grit paper, place the board deck side up and again apply masking tape to the rails. Wipe the entire top surface with a clear cloth dampened with acetone. This will pickup any remaining sanding dust and remove any oily contaminate on the surface. If you plan to add any color graphics to your board, apply them at this time using carefully applied masking tape and opaque pigments added to laminating resin . Allow the pigmented resin to set firmly before proceeding.

36. The final finish coat is ideally performed with temperature near 75° F, and there should be no air draft present. Catalyze one pint of finishing resin. Work the resin over the board just as you did with the sanding resin. You will note that the finishing resin is thinner than the sanding resin. The idea is to just cover all the scratches left by the 100 grit paper. The ideal gel time on the board for the finish coat is about 14-18 minutes. At 75° F you will probably need to use about 1½% catalyst hardener (see catalyzation chart). Cover the deckside completely and the tail fin(s), with one resin batch. Watch for brush hairs in the coating. Remove them with tweezers before the resin gels. Allow the resin to gel, then remove the masking tape. When the resin sets firmly, turn the board over. Re-apply masking tape at the rails about ¼" above the deck-side masking tape line, so that the bottom-side coat will just overlap the deck-side coat. Catalyze another pint of finishing resin and finish-coat the bottomside of the board. Remembering to use long, light brush strokes at the very end of the resin application. Remove the masking tape after the resin gels. Allow the resin to fully cure before proceeding.

37. Finishing resin dries with a semi-gloss finish which can be transformed into an extremely high gloss finish by wet sanding and polishing. Wet sand the entire surface by hand, using 400 grit and then 600 grit Wet-and-Dry silicon carbide sandpaper. Wash the surboard down carefully with water and a clean rag when you change grit sizes. All of the wax present on the surface must be removed or the surface will not polish properly.

38. By hand, or with a power buffer, polish the entire board, first with a heavy duty type fiberglass buffing compound and finally with a fine polish (i.e. Gerisch Nu Glass Fiberglass Polish). When using a power buffer, constantly move the buffer so as not to burn the surface. Buffer speed should not exceed 2400 RPM.

How to Measure and Mix
Catalyst into Resins

1. Always wear eye protection when mixing resin and catalyst. *Catalyst can cause blindness!* - even after it is mixed with the resin.

2. Resin should be in 65°F-75 of temperature range when mixed - do not leave it in the hot sun or cold areas prior to use.

3. Refer to the resin container or to the more detailed chart following to determine how much catalyst is required for the batch size you wish to catalyze.

4. Air temperature and resin temperature greatly influence resin pot life, gel time and cure time. Make adjustments to air temperature as noted on the resin container.

5. Pour the desired amount of resin into the mixing bucket. Select the catalyst measuring unit of your choice - (drops per oz., -cc/Ml, fl. ozs., teaspoons, or tablespoons.)

6. Drops (for small batches only) may be dispensed directly into resin. One oz. calibrated measuring cups are very handy for measuring the other units of measure. Pour the catalyst into the center of the resin mass.

7. Stir the resin *thoroughly* with a clean mixing stick, but avoid whipping air into the resin. *Scrape the sides of the container* to assure a complete mix.

8. Catalyzed resin in a mix bucket will always gel quicker than the same resin spread out in a coating or lamination. The larger the batch is, the faster it will gel in the mix bucket. Never return catalyzed resin to the original container.

Some good advice: Since a number of variables can affect resin pot life, it is always a good idea to pre-test the gel time. Catalyze a small quantity of resin (2-4 oz.) and apply 25% of it on a piece of scrap material. Check the gel time of the portion in the cup and in a spread out portion. This will provide you with a good approximation of how much working time you will have when you apply the first batch of resin to your project. Expect a somewhat shorter potlife with the larger batch. When making gel time adjustments never use less than ½% or more than 2% catalyst (see chart). Do not attempt to apply resins at temperatures below 60%F or above 90°F.

CATALYST/HARDENER CONCENTRATION CHART
volume of catalyst to be used with Polyester Resins
M.E.K. Peroxide (2) - Percent by Weight

Resin (1) Volume	½%			¾%			1%			1½%			2%		
	cc	oz.	tbsp(3)	cc	oz.	tbsp	cc	oz.	tbsp	cc	oz.	tbsp	cc	oz.	tbsp
One Pint	3	—	—	4	1/8	—	5	1/6+	0-1	7	1/4	0-1+	9	1/3	0-2
One Pint	5	1/8+	0-1	7	1/4	0-1+	9	1/3+	0-2	14	1/2	1-0	18	5/8	1-1
One Gallon	19	5/8	1-1	28	7/8	2-0	37	1¼	2-1+	56	2	3-2	74	2 ½	5-0

Less than one pint - For resin quantities less than one pint use 7 drops (slow set), 10 drops (medium set), 13 drops (fast set) catalyst per fluid ounce of resin.

(1) One gallon polyester = 9.2 pounds
(2) Specific gravity of M.E.K. Peroxide = 1.13.
(3) FIRST NUMBER DENOTES TABLESPOONS AND THE SECOND TEASPOONS. For example: 0-2 means zero tablespoons and two teaspoons. A plus means increase the amount slightly over that which is indicated.

ORGANIC PEROXIDE, KEEP AWAY FROM FIRE AND HEAT.

Store in original closed container in cool place. Protect from direct sunlight, heat, sparks and open flames. Do not add to hot materials. PREVENT CONTAMINATION with foreign materials, especially readily oxidizable materials and accelerators.

IN CASE OF ACCIDENTAL CONTACT:

With skin: Wash immediately with soap and water.
With eyes: Flush immediately with large amounts of water for 15 minutes and call physician.
If Swallowed: Take large quantities of milk or water and immediately call physician.
If Inhaled: Call Physician.

SAFETY

When working with fiberglass materials and resins, safety CAN-NOT be overstressed. To make this safety section a quick reference tool, we have made a list of things to do and not to do so that the reader can easily refer to this section before and during his work. Emergency care information is provided below. PLEASE READ CAREFULLY.

1. ALWAYS read instructions carefully and follow them to the letter on any product you may be using.

2. Do NOT smoke while working with fiberglass and resin, or any solvents. Avoid all open flames in the working area, *especially pilot lights on appliances.*

3. ALWAYS work in a well-ventilated area. If necessary, set up some slow speed fans to insure a complete movement of air. Avoid breathing of fumes from resins, solvents, catalysts and other accessory chemicals.

4. Wear eye-protective gear such as glasses, goggles, or a face mask. Wear a respiratory or protective mask when sanding, spray painting, or when working with fillers such as chopped fibers, microballons, fumed silica (Cab-O-Sil), etc. Keep first-aid information near work area. *Keep an instant source of eye wash water nearby.*

5. Use disposable plastic or rubber gloves and protective clothing when working with resins.

6. If resin, catalyst hardener, pigment, etc., comes in contact with the skin, *wash immediately* with soap and water or Gerisch Bio-Seven Resin Cleaner. Wash hands and other exposed areas when stopping work or before eating or smoking.

7. Do NOT mix cobalt accelerator directly with MEK peroxide catalyst as a violent reaction and/or explosion will occur. Also do not mix MEK peroxide catalyst with acetone.

8. Do NOT try home remedies if you develop toxic symptoms or extreme dermatitis. See a physician and explain what chemicals you have been working with.

9. Dispose of gelled resin properly by dispersing it well over a broad area. Concentrated resin which has begun to cure can get hot enough to ignite. Do NOT throw into trash barrels until fully cured if you cannot dump the gelling resin.

10. Watch out for children, pets and other unknowledgeable people who may enter into the work area where resins and solvents are being used.

11. Keep a FIRST AID kit handy, and try not to work alone where you may be remote from assistance if you need it.

12. DON'T LET ALL THESE SAFETY REQUIREMENTS SCARE YOU OUT OF WORKING WITH FIBERGLASS MATERIALS AND RESINS. THE EXPERIENCE CAN BE REWARDING IF YOU ARE CAREFUL.

Specific Chemical Safety Information

BEFORE USING - Carefully read all cautionary statements on the containers. WEAR EYE PROTECTION WHEN USING RESIN OR CATALYST!

Polyester Resin-Contains styrene monomer. Warning! Harmful if inhaled or swallowed. May cause irritation of skin, eyes, nose, or throat. Keep away from heat, sparks, and open flame. No smoking. Avoid breathing vapor or spray mist. Use only with adequate ventilation. Keep container closed when not in use. Avoid contact with eyes, skin, or clothing. Wash after handling. Wash clothing before reuse. Discard contaminated shoes. DO NOT SWALLOW.

First Aid-On contact, flush eyes or skin with plenty of water for at least 15 minutes. Remove contaminated shoes and clothing. If inhaled, remove to fresh air. If not breathing, give artificial respiration; a trained person should administer oxygen. If swallowed, induce vomiting. CALL A PHYSICIAN. Keep out of reach of children.

Catalyst Hardener-DANGER! METHYL ETHYL KETONE PEROXIDE IN DIMETHYL PHTHALATE. Strong irritant, corrosive to eyes. *May cause permanent blindness!* Organic Peroxide. Keep Away From Fire and Heat. Store in original closed container in cool place. Protect from direct sunlight, heat, sparks and open flames. Do not add to hot materials. Prevent contamination with foreign materials, especially readily oxidizable materials and accelerators. Do not reuse containers. Dispose of Safely.

With Skin-Wash immediately with soap and water.

With Eyes-Flush immediately (seconds count!) with large amounts of water for 30 minutes and call a physician.

If Swallowed-Take large quantities of milk or water and immediately call a physician.

If Inhaled-Call Physician immediately.

KEEP OUT OF REACH OF CHILDREN.

Acetone-Danger! Poison! Keep container closed when not in use. If swallowed, do not induce vomiting. CALL PHYSICIAN IMMEDIATELY. Remove patient to fresh air, but have him lie down and keep warm. Cover eyes to exclude light. In case of contact with eyes, flood repeatedly with water. Do not transfer to unlabelled containers. EXTREMELY FLAMMABLE! KEEP AWAY FROM HEAT, SPARKS,

AND OPEN FLAME. Close container after each use. Avoid prolonged or repeated breathing of vapor or contact with skin. Before eating or smoking and after using, wash hands thoroughly. Do not take internally. Use only with adequate ventilation. Keep out of reach of children. Store chemicals in a cool place, but not in a food refrigerator.

TROUBLE SHOOTING GUIDE

Laminating Resins

Problem	Possible Cause	Items to check/ Solution/Prevention
Slow cure (entire laminate)	1. Catalyst level too low. 2. If in low temperature conditions (60-65°F) laminate may be too thin.	1. Check catalyst/hardener concentration chart. 2. Increase catalyst and/or laminate thickness.
Uncured spots	1. Poor catalyst mix. 2. Catalyst not added to all resin batches. 3. Water, oil or contaminate in substrate, moisture in fiberglass fabric.	1. Review section (I). 2. Add catalyst to each batch. 3. Solvent wash off contaminate. Allow to dry before applying resin. Don't use moist fiberglass fabrics.
Air bubbles in laminate	1. Poor squeegee or rollout job.	1. Make greater effort to remove bubbles before resin gels.
Air patches, dry sections under fiberglass	1. Glass lifted prior to resin gel. 2. Resin drained out of laminate on vertical. 3. Too little resin in laminate.	1. Continue to spot-roll or dab with brush, areas showing signs of lifting until resin gels. 2. Add Gerisch Resin Thick to resin, or work project horizontally. 3. Add more resin to trouble spots prior to gel. 4. Take more care to "wet" all the glass.
Hot spots	1. Multiple laminates applied too rapidly or too thick in spots. 2. Improper catalyst mix.	1. Space out time between laminate layer applications. 2. Mix catalyst thoroughly.

Laminating Resins con't.

Problem	Possible Cause	Items to check/ Solution/Prevention
Resin cracks	1. Catalyst level too high.	1. Reduce catalyst level.
	2. Resin % too high -puddles.	2. Use less resin.
Glass pickup on rollers	1. Dirty rollers.	1. Clean rollers in clean acetone.
	2. Rolling too fast.	2. Slow down.
	3. Resin sticky due to styrene evaporation.	3. Apply fresh resin in smaller batches more frequently.
	4. Glass % too high.	4. Use more resin.
Warpage of parts.	1. Laminate applied to a substrate material too thin to resist normal resin shrink force.	1. Increase thickness or stiffness of substrate material.
	2. Excess catalyst causing excess shrink, warp.	2. Reduce catalyst %.

Sanding and Finishing Resins

Problem	Possible Cause	Items to check/ Solution/Prevention
Entire surface sticky - not curing.	1. Application too thin.	1. Apply thicker resin coat.
	2. Catalyst % too low.	2. Increase catalyst %.
	3. If pigment used - too much was added.	3. Do not exceed 1 oz. pigment per qt. resin.
	4. Ambient temperature too low.	4. 75°F - best temp. for finish work.
Spotty cure (Some areas show waxy surface with good cure - others are glossy and sticky.)	1. Vertical application.	1. Set surface in horizontal position before applying resin.
	2. Gel time too long.	2. Increase catalyst.
	3. Temperature too low.	3. Apply at warmer temperature.
	4. Resin applied in direct sunlight.	4. Do not apply in direct sun.

Sanding and Finishing Resins con't.

Problem	Possible Cause	Items to check/ Solution/Prevention
Air bubbles in finish coat.	1. Gel time too fast 2. Ambient temperature too warm. 3. Resin "whipped" too much during mixing.	1. Reduce catalyst. 2. Reduce catalyst or apply in cooler weather. 3. Slow down mixing motion, but be sure mix is complete.
Ripples or "orange peel" texture on surface of finish coat.	1. Too much catalyst. 2. Weather too hot. 3. Resin applied in direct sun. 4. Too much air motion over surface.	1. Reduce catalyst. 2. Apply in cooler weather. 3. Work in a shaded area. 4. Eliminate fast moving air, but maintain adequate ventilation.
"Fisheyes" separations in finish coat.	1. Entire substrate is contaminated with oily substrate. 2. Substrate oil contamination, spots.	1. There is no practical solution for this condition unless all traces of oil can be removed by deep sanding. 2. Sand surface, solvent (acetone) wash - try again.
Deep surface scratches - will not buff out	1. Proper sanding grit sequence was not followed. 2. Grit contamination.	1. Don't short cut sanding steps. 2. Wash part between grit size changes.
Excessive brush marks in finish coat	1. Too much pressure applied with brush. 2. Gel time too fast.	1. Use *light* long strokes. 2. Decrease catalyst %. Allow more time for resin to self level before gel after brushing.

Fiber Reinforced Plastics Glossary

Accelerator – Material used in conjuction with a catalyst to produce and hasten the internal heat reaction in the liquid resin for cure. The accelerator used in most polyester resins for fiberglass work is cobalt napthanate, usually referred to as "cobalt." Almost all resins sold today already contain the required amount of accelerator.

Acetone – A highly flammable and toxic cleaning fluid used to remove uncured resin from tools and clothing.

Activator – see Accelerator

Air-Inhibited Resin – A resin which will not completely cure or "set up" in the presence of air. Polyester resin which does not contain wax is classed as "air inhibited."

Catalyst – Material added to resin to make it cure rapidly by oxidation with an accelerator as in polyester resins. This causes the heat which in turn cures the resin. The catalyst used in most polyester resins is methyl ethyl ketone peroxide, usually referred to as "M-E-K" peroxide - *not to be confused with MEK solvent.*

Chopper Gun – A special spray gun used for spray-up laminating which chops predetermined lengths of fiberglass roving or strands, and deposits them together with catalyzed resin at the same time onto the mold surface.

Colbalt Napthanate – An accelerator used in polyester resin. Also an additive that will allow resin to be used at lower temperatures (see accelerator).

Composite – Type of construction using two or more different materials, such as resin and fiberglass material.

Crazing – Hairline cracks either within or on the surface of fiberglass laminates, caused by stresses generated by excessive heat during cure, removal from the mold, impact, or flexing.

Cure – The changing of the liquid resin to a solid state. Once the resin begins to cure, the process cannot be reversed. The technical term for cure is "polymerization."

Cure Time – The time required for the liquid resin to reach a point when it is hard enough to have other processes performed with it, such as sanding or finishing, or when it is no longer "tacky" or "sticky." Technically, it is the time required for the resin to reach a "polymerized state" after the catalyst has been added.

Delamination – Separation or failure of the bond in laminate layers from each other or from another surface material.

"DMA" – Dimethylanaline, a promoter used in resins.

E-Glass – A specific glass composition formula commonly used for boat and surfboard building reinforcements.

Epoxy Resin – Thermosetting resins in boat work of a two-part type, that when combined, cure and form into an extremely hard and tough product. They will adhere better and shrink less than polyester resins, have generally greater strength, although they are much more expensive.

Exothermic Heat – The heat given off by the resin developed internally during the curing process, or "polymerization." It is caused by the reaction of the accelerator and the catalyst when mixed in polyester resins, and by the hardener in epoxy resins.

Feather Edge – The process of tapering the edge of a resin-saturated fiberglass material to blend with the adjoining surface, as opposed to having an abrupt edge.

Female Mold – The type of mold commonly used in production fiberglass boatbuilding where the outer surface of the molded part contacts, and is formed by, the surface of the female mold.

Fiberglass – Fiber similar to those of other fabrics, but made from glass. Materials made from fiberglass fibers in boat work include cloth fabrics, rovings and woven rovings, uni-directional rovings, and various mats.

Filament – A hair-like particle or "rod" of glass used to make fiberglass. Filament can be made in virtually an endless length.

Filler – Material added to resin to extend the volume or change the qualities of the resin.

Fillet – A rounded filling on an inside corner or angle.

Finish – The surface cleaning treatment applied to the glass fibers after weaving them into cloth in order to allow the resin to flow freely around and adhere to them. The finish determines the quality of the adhesion between the glass and the resin. The common finishes for fiberglass in boat work are chrome ("Volan") or silane finish.

Finishing Resin – A polyester resin containing wax surfacing agent which floats to the surface to exclude the air from the resin surface, thereby allowing it to cure or "set up."

Fire-Retardant Resin – Resin type which has been formulated with chemicals to reduce or nearly eliminate its tendency to burn when once cured or "polymerized." It should be noted that fire retardant resins are not "fire proof."

Foam – In boat work this term usually refers to rigid foam plastics of three types: polystyrene ("styrofoam"), polyurethane (including the pour-in-place type), and polyvinyl chloride (PVC).

"FRP" – Fiber Reinforced Plastic.

Gel/Gelation – The partial cure of polyester resin to a semi-solid or "jelly-like" state.

Gel Coat – A thin surface coat of specially formulated polyester resin used as the surface covering on hulls made using the female mold process and usually applied by spraying.

Gel Time – The time it takes to change the liquid resin to a non-flowing gel. Also, the time available for working the resin once applied. See also Pot Life.

Glass Content/Glass-Resin Ratio – The amount of fiberglass reinforcing material in a laminate compared to the amount of resin. Glass content assumes that sufficient resin exists to convert the materials into a stiff, structural laminiate.

Hand Lay Up – The application of fiberglass laminates using manual labor usually in a female mold to produce a boat hull or related structure.

Hardener – See Catalyst. The catalyst for epoxy resins is commonly called the "hardener."

Inhibitor – An additive to polyester resin which retards curing or polymerization, thereby extending the shelf life of the resin. It also influences gel time and exothermic heat.

Isophthalic ("Iso") Resin – Isophthalic acid based polyester resin which has somewhat higher physical properties than orthophthalic resins, but also considered a "general purpose" resin.

"Kevlar" – A proprietary Aramid fiber made by Du Pont Chemical for making reinforcing materials.

Laminating Resin – A polyester resin that will not completely cure tack-free in the presence of air.

Lamination – The laying on of layers of fiberglass materials and resin, much like the build-up of plywood laminations. The layers of material are bonded together with resin to form the laminate.

Lap Joint – A joint made by positioning one material over another end-to-end or side-by-side as opposed to a butt joint. The joint consists of two layers of material.

Lay Up – The placing of fiberglass reinforcing materials onto the mold surface and applying the resin to form the completed laminate.

Male Mold – The type of mold where a part is made up over the mold instead of inside the mold, with the inner surface of the molded part against the mold surface.

Mat – Randomly oriented strands of glass fibers formed into a felt and held together with a binder, usually of thinned polyester resin in a powder-like form. Most mat material used in boat work is the chopped-strand type.

"M-E-K-P" – Methyl ethyl ketone peroxide, a catalyst commonly used for polyester resin.

M.E.K. Solvent – A highly flammable and toxic cleaning fluid used to remove uncured resin from tools and clothing.

"Microballoons" - "Microspheres" – Any of the several available types of microscopic gas filled balloons or balloon aggregates. They may be composed of glass, phenolic, Saran® or various silicates. When added to resins they make light weight patching pastes sometimes referred to as "syntactic foams."

Mold Release – see Parting Agent.

Monomer – The technical word for a compound which is usually in liquid form and has the ability to be changed into a polymer (solid form), or "polymerized." Styrene is a common monomer used in polyester resins.

Non-Air-Inhibited Resin – A resin which will completely cure or "set up" in the presence of air. A surfacing agent (usually wax) is added to the resin which floats to the surface to exclude the air from the resin surface, thereby allowing it to cure or "polymerize."

Orthophthalic ("Ortho") Resin – Orthophthalic acid based polyester resin. Considered a "general purpose" resin.

Parting Agent – Any material used to coat the mold to prevent the molded part from sticking when being removed, or a material used to keep resin from sticking to any part of the work. Common release agents are wax, polyvinyl alcohol (PVA), cellophane, glass, and "Formica." Wax and PVA are commonly used in female mold factory production boat-building.

Plug – A male form identical in shape to the finished object over which a female mold is fabricated.

Polyester Resin – Thermosetting resins which require the addition of a catalyst and accelerator to effect the cure. This type of resin is used for most boat work. See also Epoxy Resin.

Polymerization – The chemical reaction of monomer, usually from a liquid state to a solid state. See also Cure.

Porosity – The formation of undesirable clusters of air bubbles in the surface or body of a laminate.

Post-Cure – Exposure of the cured resin to higher temperatures than during curing in order to obtain a more complete cure or more rapid cure.

Pot Life – The length of time that a catalyzed resin remains workable while in a container until it must be discarded. Similar to Gel Time (see also) except that gel time refers to the resin on the surface.

Print-Through – The weave or pattern of reinforcing material showing through the exterior surface or gel coat of a laminate.

Promoter – See Accelerator.

Promoted Resin – Polyester resin to which an accelerator has been added. Resin which does not have accelerator is said to be "unpromoted." Resin which has the promoter added before the user adds the catalyst is said to be "pre-promoted."

Release Agent – See Parting Agent.

Resin – A liquid plastic substance about the consistency of honey and used in conjuction with fiberglass materials to form a laminate. In boat work, polyester and epoxy resins are the common types.

Resin Rich – An area, especially in a laminate, where too much resin has been applied in relation to the fiberglass reinforcing material. The opposite of a Dry Spot or "resin starved" area. Also referred to as a "resin pocket" and "resin streak."

Roving – Continuous strands of glass fibers grouped together to form an untwisted yarn or rope. Rovings are commonly used for chopper gun spray-up laminates and to form woven rovings.

Sandwich Construction – A type of fiberglass construction which resembles a sandwich consisting of relatively dense but high-strength facings bonded to a less dense but thicker intermediate material or "core." Core materials in boat work include foams, balsa, lumber, and plywood.

Shelf Life – The length of time an uncatalyzed resin remains usable while stored in a sealed container. Most polyester resins have a shelf life of from six months to one year.

S-Glass – A particular glass formula having higher strength properties than E-Glass.

Sizing – The surface treatment on glass fibers during the fiber forming operation which aids in machine manufacture as well as allowing the resin to adhere to the fibers in use, as is the case with mats and rovings. Sizing is similar to Finish for cloth, but because mats and rovings are not "dirtied" by the weaving process, no finish is required.

Spray-up – In boat work, a method of fiberglass lay up performed with a Chopper Gun (see also) which cuts and deposits fiberglass rovings and catalyzed resin onto the mold surface. See also Hand Lay Up.

Styrene – A water-thin liquid hydrocarbon monomer which is the primary ingredient of polyester resin. Also can be used as a thinner of polyester resin, to a limited extent.

Substrate – A material that provides a supporting surface for other materials.

Surfacing Agent – Material added to polyester resin or used in association with it to prevent air from reaching the surface of polyester resin so the resin can cure. Surfacing agent is commonly paraffin wax in a solution.

Surfacing Mat-A lightweight but rather stiff mat used next to the gel coat in a female mold to improve surface appearance of the final product as well as minimize water absorption.

Syntactic Foam-Resin which has been made lower in denisty, light in weight, less viscous, and generally "stretched out" by the addition of fillers-usually microspheres.

Thermoplastic Resin-A type of resin which can be repeatedly softened or reformed by the application of heat, and can be rehardened by cooling. This type of resin is not used in fiberglass work.

Thermosetting Resin-A type of resin which will undergo a chemical change from a liquid state as the result of the heat induced by the addition of certain materials. Once it becomes solid, it cannot be reformed by reheating. Polyester and epoxy resins are of the thermosetting type.

Thickener-Material added to resin to thicken or increase the viscosity of the resin so it will not flow as readily. A common thickener in polyester resins used for boat work is fumed silica, which helps make the resin Thixotropic.

Thinner-Material added to resin in order to thin it or lower the viscosity of the resin. There is a limit to the amount of thinner that can be added without affecting the desirable qualities of the resin. Styrene (see also) is the common thinner for polyester resin, although acetone will thin resin also, but should generally not be used for this purpose.

Thixotropic-A quality of some resins to thicken at rest but become fluid again on agitation and stirring. Thixotropic resins are used in boat work to minimize runs and sags on vertical surfaces.

Vinyl-Ester Resin-A type of polyester resin with improved physical properties, especially at elevated temperatures, over either ortho or iso polyesters.

Viscosity-The measure of the resistance of a liquid to flow. A more viscous liquid will not flow as easily as one that has less viscosity.

Warp-Along the length of fabric or material.

Weft-Across the width of fabric or material.

Wet Out-The ability of a resin to quickly saturate the fiberglass material.

Wicking – The travel of moisture or water through fibers in a laminate not toally wetted out or encapsulated with resin.

Woven Roving – Fiberglass rovings woven into a coarse fabric much heavier than, but similar to, plain square weave cloth fabric.

Essential Surfing Glossary

Ankle strap – secures leash to ankle

angle off – gradually descending the face of the wave toward the left or right

acetone – a cleaning solvent for catalized/uncatalized resin

backwash – a wave reflected back out to sea

backside – riding with one's back to the wave

belly – a convex bottom contour

blank – the foam core of a surfboard that the shaper starts out with

catalyst – added to resin to make it harden

cavitation – the rapid formation and collapse of vapor pockets in a flowing liquid in regions of very low pressure; occurs on one side of a fin disrupting control

chine rails – rails that are faceted or beveled rather than rounded

close-out – a wave that breaks all at once/not suitable for surfing

cord – leash

concave – a concave bottom contour

crest – the tallest part of the wave which usually breaks first

delamination – a separation of layers laminated together – most often a failure of the foam/fiberglass bond

domed deck – (also referred to as a crowned deck) a rounded, rather than flat deck that provides a thicker stringer and increased foam volume (flotation) down the center of the board

down-the-line – where the surfer maneuvers to on a breaking wave

drop in – taking off on a wave or riding from the top of the wave straight to the bottom

east swell – a swell that moves from the east to the west

east wind – a wind that blows from the east to the west

ebb – a tide that is going from high to low

fetch – the amount of area that the wind has to act upon the water during the creation of waves and swell

fiberglass – glass fibers woven into a cloth which is saturated with resin, used to strengthen the exterior of a blank

fin – used for directional stability on the bottom of the surfboard

fin box – a plastic channel that the fin slides into

flood – a tide that is going from low to high

foil – the distribution of foam; lengthwise thickness flow of a blank; thickness cross section of a fin

frontside–riding while facing the wave

glassing–laminating fiberglass cloth with resin to a shaped blank

glassy–smooth, calm water surface; no presence of wind

gloss–the thin final coat of resin that is buffed out

goofy foot–riding a surfboard with your right foot forward, left foot back

grit cloth–grit coated screen used for blending rail contours when shaping foam

hard rail–a rail with a sharper corner, and a more defined edge

hot coat–the resin layer which is sanded to blend and refine contours of the board (also refered to as the sand coat)

impact zone–the area where the wave first breaks

juice–the power of the wave

kevlar–an aramid fiber cloth

kick–rocker of the nose area

kickout–an abrupt turn used to get out of a wave

laminating–glassing

lap line–the edge of laminated fiberglass cloth (usually trimmed)

leash–cord secures surfer to surfboard

left–a wave that breaks from left to right as viewed from shore

lip–the part of the wave that comes over first when the wave breaks

lift–the force created when flow is faster across one side of an asymmetrical foil than another

locals–surfers that live in an area or surf it the most

lull–the period between sets when the waves are smaller or nonexistent

north swell–a swell that moves from north to south

north wind–a wind that blows from north to south

nose–front third of a surfboard

nose ride–standing and riding on the nose

offshore–a wind that blows from land to sea

onshore–a wind that blows from sea to land

outside–an area beyond which most set waves break

peak–the crest or first part of the wave to break

pearling–nose catches in the water

pigment–an opaque coloring agent for resin

planer–a power tool used to remove foam from blanks quickly and easily

planing surface–a surface that skims on top of the water; the bottom of the surfboard

prone out–to straighten out in front of the wave and lay down on your board

proplugs–Dr. Scott's ear plugs for the prevention of surfer's ear

quiver–a set of surfboards to accommodate varying conditions and wave sizes

rail/rail line–the outside edge of the surfboard

rail radii–the curve that joins the top and bottom of the surfboard

rail saver–a nylon strap used to prevent the leash from tearing into the rail

rake–the way fin area is arranged in relation to the base

respirator–a mask used to filter toxic fumes and dust from the air

regular foot–riding a surfboard with your left foot forward, right foot back

right–a wave that breaks right to left as viewed from shore

rocker–lengthwise bottom curvature of a surfboard

rip–a current in the ocean; to surf radically

sand coat–the resin layer which is sanded to blend and refine contours of the board (also refered to as the hot coat)

screw foot–riding a surfboard with your right foot forward, left foot back

sets–largest waves to come through on a particular day

shape–the foam blank as completed by the shaper

shaper–craftsman who shapes foam

shoulder–the part of the wave which hasn't broken yet

skeg–fin

soft rail–a rounder rail with a softer, less defined edge

soup–whitewater

south swell–a swell that moves from south to north

south wind–a wind that blows from south to north

speed bead–a resin ridge near the rail on the bottom to direct water flow and increase speed

squeegee–a rubber tool used to force/saturate resin into fiberglass cloth

stoked–the great enthusiasm one feels from surfing

straighten off–to straighten out in front of the whitewater to escape the wave

stinger–shifts in the template that alter the rail line

stringer–a strip of wood that runs down the middle of the blank

styrene–a resin thinner

surfer's ear – a condition affecting surfers where bony growth closes the ear canal

swell – waves caused by a common storm system

surform – a hand plane used on foam

surf cord – leash which attaches surfer to surfboard

switch-stance – the ability to ride frontside on both rights and lefts

tail – rear third of surfboard; type of tail design

template – sillouhette of a surfboard top or bottom

tint – a transparent coloring agent for resin

trim – orienting yourself on the surfboard so it can plane as fast as possible

trough – bottom of the wave

tube – tunnel inside a breaking wave

v – flat angled bottom contour; not curved

venturi effect – a property of fluids that causes a speed increase as they flow from a larger area through a smaller one

warp – strands that run the length of fiberglass cloth

wax – rubbed on the deck of a surfboard for traction

welp – (also referred to as fill) strands that run the width of fiberglass cloth

wetsuit – a rubber suit, snugly fit to allow a thin layer of water to enter which is warmed by body heat and keeps the user warm

west swell – a swell that travels from west to east

west wind – a wind that blows from west to east

whitewater – the turbulence resulting from a collapsed wave

wings/bump wings – shifts in the template that alter the rail line

wipeout – falling off the surfboard

LIST OF CONTRIBUTORS

Aleeda Wetsuits
208 Main Street
Huntington Beach, California 92648
(714) 960-7678

Charley Baldwin – Inlet Charley's Surfshop
510 Flagler Ave.
New Smyrna, Florida 32069
(904) 423-2317

Tim Bessell
423 West Bourne
La Jolla, California 92037
(619) 456-2591

George Bredehoft – Progressive Curves
(415) 665-7528

Dick Brewer Surfboards – Steve Morgan
P.O. Box 72
Maunaloa, Molokai, Hawaii 96770
(808) 826-6644

Brian Bulkley
P.O. Box 721
South Laguna, California 92677
(714) 494-0178

Bill Caster Memorial Surfboards
c/o Diamond Glassing (619) 566-7629 and
Hank Warner (619) 578-2314

Channel Island Surf Shop – Al Merrick
29 State Street
Santa Barbara, California 93101
(805) 966-7213

Clark Foam – Gordon Clark, Dick Morales, Matt Barker
25887 Crown Valley Parkway
South Laguna, California 92677
(714) 582-1431

Doc's Pro Plugs – Ocean @ Earth - Hotline
Brenda Scott Rogers
P.O. Box 262
Capitola, California 95010
(408) 462-5919 / 425-4809

Eaton Enterprises – Mike Eaton
3979 La Salle Street
San Diego, California 92110
(619) 224-5603

Gerisch Products, Inc. – Robert Pettijohn
20814 S. Normandie Ave.
Torrance, California 90502
(213) 320-5479

Gordon and Smith Surfboards
7081 Consolidated Way
San Diego, California 92121-2604
(619) 549-2690

Hot Stuff Surfboards – Tom Eberly
P.O. Box 626
Carlsbad, California 92008
(619) 438-0556

Lance Carson Surfboards – Lance Carson
P.O. Box 1205
Pacific Palisades, California 90272
(213) 459-1159

Linden Surfboards – Gary Linden
1027 S. Cleveland St.
Oceanside, California 92054
(619) 722-8956

Lite Composite Systems – Rod, Todd
1000 Cindy Lane
Carpinteria, California 93013
(805) 684-5432, 963-2619

Lite Wave – Tom Williams
P.O. Box 5294
Santa Barbara, California 93108
(805) 648-0611

Matt Kechele Surfboards – Matt Kechele
P.O. Box 374
Cocoa Beach, Florida 32931
(305) 783-7412

Kno-Naw Corp. – John Kershaw
(619) 722-8949

Nectar Surfboards – Gary MacNabb
2571 S. Hwy. 101
Cardiff-By-The-Sea, California 92007
(619) 753-6649

Nose Guard Hawaii - Surf Co. Hawaii, Inc.
98-029 Hekaka St., #14
Aiea, Hawaii 96701
(808) 488-5996

NSSA - National Scholastic Surfing Association
Carolyn Adams and Chuck Allen
P.O. Box 495
Huntington Beach, California 92648
(714) 841-3254

O'Neill Wetsuits – Tom Carmody
(408) 475-7500

Power Stroke Gloves – Jon Kemp
P.O. Box 390355
Kailua-Kona, Hawaii 96739
(808) 326-7286

Rusty Surfboards – Rusty Preisendorfer
5171 C Santa Fe Street
San Diego, California 92109
(619) 581-2277, 581-2278

R.P. Designs – Robin Prodanovich
P.O. Box 7075
San Diego, California 92107
(619) 226-7667

Project Wipe Out, Hoag Memorial Hospital Presbyterian
301 Newport Boulevard, Box Y
Newport Beach, California 92663
(714) 760-5880

Pro-Lite Surfboard Protection Equipment
Dave Neilsen
177 Riverside Drive, Suite F
Newport Beach, California 92663
(714) 631-3477

Rainbow Fin Company – Glen DeWitt
P.O. Box 191 MBA
Watsonville, California 95076
(408) 728-2998

Rip Curl Wetsuits – Ray Thomas
(714) 498-4920

Ron Romanosky Kneeboards
P.O. Box 2648
Costa Mesa, California 92628
(714) 541-8541

Saxon Holt Photography – Saxon Holt
601 - 22nd Street
San Francisco, California 94107
(415) 695-7788

Schroff Surfboards – Peter Schroff
(714) 645-2614

Seatrend Sailboards – Randy French
1053 17th Avenue
Santa Cruz, California 95062
(408) 462-3633

Speedskin - Verachem Corp. – Jason Pallas
17850 Maumee
Grosse Pointe, MI 48230
(313) 884-8008

Stewart Surfboards – Bill Stewart
2102 South El Camino Real
San Clemente, California 92672
(714) 492-1085

Surf Design Custom Sailboards – Larry McElheny
P.O. Box 491
Haleiwa, Hawaii 96712
(808) 638-8484

S.M.A. – Surfer's Medical Association
Dr. Mark Renneker – "Doc Hazard"
2396 Great Highway/48th Avenue
San Francisco, California 94116
(415) 664-7027

Surfrider Foundation
P.O. Box 2704 #86
Huntington Beach, California 92647
(714) 846-3462

Town & Country Surfboards
P.O. Box 730
Pearl City, Hawaii 96782
(808) 455-3767

U.S.S.F. – United States Surfing Federation
Dr. Colin J. Couture
11 Adams Pt. Road
Barrington, Rhode Island 02806
(617) 336-9536/(401) 245-5067

The U.S.S.F. is the governing body for amateur surfing in the United States. Five
regional surfing associations; ESA (Eastern), GSA (Gulf), TSA (Texas), WSA
(Western), HSA (Hawaiian) and two specialty organizations; the NSSA-National
Scholastic Surfing Association and W.I.S.A.-Women's International Surfing Association. Contact the USSF for informtion.

Victoria Skimboards–Tex and Lynn Haines
2955 Laguna Canyon Road
Laguna Beach, California 92651
(714) 494-0059
Webs The Glove
P.O. Box 2712
Huntington Beach, California 92647
(714) 895-4358
William Peterson, O.D.
(Dr. Petersen's office is also the S.M.A. reference library)
34127 Coast Highway
Dana Point, California 92629
(714) 661-1181
Wise Surfboards–Bob Wise
3149 Vicente Street
San Francisco, California 94116
(415) 665-7745

Bibliography

Ding Repair Scriptures
By George Colendich
Village Green Publications
6362 Glenhaven Road, Soquel, California 95073

Surfing Fundamentals
By Nat Young
Palm Beach Press
40 Ocean Road, Palm Beach, Palm Beach NSW 2108

Waves and Beaches
By Willard Bascom
Anchor Books, Doubleday & Co., Inc.
Garden City, New York

This book may be ordered by sending
Eleven Dollars (which covers the price of
the book plus shipping and handling) to:

George Orbelian
417 Dewey Boulevard
San Francisco, California 94116